Out of the Wreckage

Out of the Wreckage

A New Politics for an Age of Crisis

George Monbiot

VERSO
London • New York

This paperback edition first published by Verso 2018
First published by Verso 2017
© George Monbiot 2017, 2018

Figures from Kate Raworth's *Doughnut Economics* and Paul
Samuelson's *Economics* are reproduced with permission, for
which the author and publisher express their gratitude.

The moral rights of the author have been asserted

5 7 9 10 8 6 4

Verso
UK: 6 Meard Street, London W1F 0EG
US: 20 Jay Street, Suite 1010, Brooklyn, NY 11201
versobooks.com

Verso is the imprint of New Left Books

ISBN-13: 978-1-78663-289-0
ISBN-13: 978-1-78663-291-3 (US EBK)
ISBN-13: 978-1-78663-290-6 (UK EBK)

British Library Cataloguing in Publication Data
A catalogue record for this book is available from the British Library

The Library of Congress Has Cataloged the Hardback Edition as Follows:

Names: Monbiot, George, 1963– author.
Title: Out of the wreckage : a new politics for an age of crisis / George
  Monbiot.
Description: Brooklyn, NY : Verso, 2017. | Includes bibliographical
  references and index. |
Identifiers: LCCN 2017025514 (print) | LCCN 2017045885 (ebook) | ISBN
  9781786632913 (E-book) | ISBN 9781786632883 (hardback)
Subjects: LCSH: Political sociology. | Economics – Sociological aspects. |
  Political participation. | Direct democracy. | BISAC: POLITICAL SCIENCE /
  Political Process / General. | SOCIAL SCIENCE / Anthropology / Cultural. |
  NATURE / Environmental Conservation & Protection.
Classification: LCC JA76 (ebook) | LCC JA76 .M59 2017 (print) | DDC
  306.2 – dc23
LC record available at https://lccn.loc.gov/2017025514

Typeset in Fournier MT by Hewer Text Ltd, Edinburgh
Printed and bound by CPI Group (UK) Ltd, Croydon, CR0 4YY

To Rebecca, Hanna and Martha
With my love, and in hope of a better world.

Nations and peoples are largely the stories they feed themselves. If they tell themselves stories that are lies, they will suffer the future consequences of those lies. If they tell themselves stories that face their own truths, they will free their histories for future flowerings.

Ben Okri, *A Way of Being Free*

Contents

1

A Story of Our Times

You cannot take away someone's story without giving them a new one. It is not enough to challenge an old narrative, however outdated and discredited it may be. Change happens only when you replace it with another. When we develop the right story, and learn how to tell it, it will infect the minds of people across the political spectrum. Those who tell the stories run the world.

The old world, which once looked stable, even immutable, is collapsing. A new era has begun, loaded with hazard if we fail to respond, charged with promise if we seize the moment. Whether the systems that emerge from this rupture are better or worse than the current dispensation depends on our ability to tell a new story, a story that learns from the past, places us in the present and guides the future.

The Power of the Story

Stories are the means by which we navigate the world. They allow us to interpret its complex and contradictory signals.

We all possess a narrative instinct: an innate disposition to listen for an account of who we are and where we stand. In his illuminating book *Don't Even Think About It*, George Marshall explains that 'stories perform a fundamental cognitive function: they are the means by which the Emotional Brain makes sense of the information collected by the Rational Brain. People may hold *information* in the form of data and figures, but their *beliefs* about it are held entirely in the form of stories.'[1] When we encounter a complex issue and try to understand it, what we look for is not consistent and reliable facts but a consistent and comprehensible story. When we ask ourselves whether something 'makes sense', the 'sense' we seek is not rationality, as scientists and philosophers perceive it, but narrative fidelity. Does what we are hearing reflect the way we expect humans and the world to behave? Does it hang together? Does it progress as stories should progress?

Drawing on experimental work, Marshall shows that, even when people have been told something is fictitious, they will cling to it if it makes a good story and they have heard it often enough. Attempts to refute such stories tend only to reinforce them, as the disproof constitutes another iteration of the narrative. When we argue, 'It's not true that a shadowy clique of American politicians orchestrated the attack on the World Trade Centre', those who believe the false account hear that 'a shadowy clique of American politicians orchestrated the attack on the World Trade Centre'. The phrase 'It's not true that' carries less weight than the familiar narrative to which it is attached.

A string of facts, however well attested, has no power to correct or dislodge a powerful story. The only response it is likely to provoke is indignation: people often angrily deny facts that clash with the narrative 'truth' established in their minds.

The only thing that can displace a story is a story.

Effective stories tend to possess a number of common elements. They are easy to understand. They can be briefly summarised and quickly memorised. They are internally consistent. They concern particular characters or groups. There is a direct connection between cause and effect. They describe progress – from a beginning through a middle to an end. The end resolves the situation encountered at the beginning, with a conclusion that is positive and inspiring.

Certain stories are repeated across history and through different cultures. For example, the story of the hero setting out on a quest, encountering great hazard (often in the form of a monster), conquering it in the face of overwhelming odds, and gaining prestige, power or insight is common to cultures all over the world, some of which had no possible contact with each other. Ulysses, Beowulf, Sinbad, Sigurd, Cú Chulainn, Arjuna, St George, Lạc Long Quân and Glooskap are all variants of this universal hero. Our minds appear to be attuned not only to stories in general, but to particular stories that follow consistent patterns.

In politics, there is a recurring story that captures our attention. It goes like this:

> Disorder afflicts the land, caused by powerful and nefarious forces working against the interests of humanity. The hero – who might be one person or a group of people – revolts against this disorder, fights the nefarious forces, overcomes them despite great odds and restores order.

Stories that follow this pattern can be so powerful that they sweep all before them: even our fundamental values. For example, two of the world's best-loved and most abiding narratives – *The Lord of the Rings* and the *Narnia* series – invoke values that were familiar in the Middle Ages but are generally considered repulsive today. Disorder in these stories is characterised by the usurpation of rightful kings or their rightful heirs; justice and order rely on their restoration. We find ourselves cheering the resumption of autocracy, the destruction of industry and even, in the case of *Narnia*, the triumph of divine right over secular power.

If these stories reflected the values most people profess – democracy, independence, industrial 'progress' – the rebels would be the heroes and the hereditary rulers the villains. We overlook the conflict with our own priorities because the stories resonate so powerfully with the narrative structure for which our minds are prepared. Facts, evidence, values, beliefs: stories conquer all.

Heroes and Villains

The two most successful political stories of the twentieth century – both of which have survived into the twenty-first – are diametrically opposed to each other, but follow the same narrative pattern.

The social-democratic story explains that the world fell into disorder – characterised by the Great Depression – because of the self-seeking behaviour of an unrestrained elite. The elite's capture of both the world's wealth and the political system resulted in the impoverishment and insecurity of working people. By uniting to defend their common interests, the world's people could throw down the power of this elite, strip it of its ill-gotten gains and pool the resulting wealth for the good of all. Order and security would be restored in the form of a protective, paternalistic state, investing in public projects for the public good, generating the wealth that would guarantee a prosperous future for everyone. The ordinary people of the land – the heroes of the story – would triumph over those who had oppressed them.

The neoliberal story explains that the world fell into disorder as a result of the collectivising tendencies of the over-mighty state, exemplified by the monstrosities of Stalinism and Nazism, but evident in all forms of state planning and all attempts to engineer social outcomes. Collectivism crushes freedom, individualism and opportunity. Heroic entrepreneurs, mobilising the redeeming power of the market, would fight this enforced conformity, freeing society from the enslavement of the state. Order would be restored in the form of free markets, delivering wealth and opportunity, guaranteeing a prosperous future for everyone. The ordinary people of the land, released by the heroes of the story (the freedom-seeking entrepreneurs) would triumph over those who had oppressed them.

In the next two chapters, I will show how both stories ran into trouble, encountering problems that, if facts and evidence ruled the world, would have forced either the radical modification or abandonment of these doctrines. But because of their narrative power and a disastrous failure to develop effective countervailing stories, they have yet to be replaced. The facts changed, but our minds did not.

If the rupture is to be resolved for good rather than for ill, we need a new story. Our challenge is to produce one that is faithful to the facts, faithful to our values, and faithful to the narrative patterns to which we respond.

The Sound of Silence

Like many people who seek a generous, inclusive politics, I have been listening for such a story, waiting for its bugle call to resound, so that we can rally in the expectation of a better future. The wait continues. Most mainstream parties seek only to tweak existing narratives. This is why they often seem effete, passionless and exhausted.

Beyond the established parties, popular movements suffer, if anything, from the opposite problem. A thousand fragments of story clamour to be heard, creating, for those who stand outside, an unintelligible cacophony. Without a coherent and stabilising narrative, these movements remain reactive, disaggregated and precarious, always at risk of burnout and disillusion.

Despair is the state we fall into when our imagination fails. When we have no stories that describe the present and guide the future, hope evaporates. Political failure is, in essence, a failure of imagination.

Without a new story, a story that is positive and propositional rather than reactive and oppositional, nothing changes. With such a story, everything changes.

In seeking to develop a restorative political story around which we can gather and mobilise, we should first identify the values and principles we want to champion. This is because the stories we tell propagate the beliefs around which they are built.

I am not suggesting that those who read or watch *The Lord of the Rings* are provoked to leap from their sofas shouting 'bring back feudalism!' The story was not intended to create political change, and there has been no attempt (as far as I know) to use it to advance autocracy. But when stories are designed for a political purpose and circulated to advance this purpose, they have the power to change or strengthen our values. The most grotesque doctrines can look like common sense when embedded in a compelling narrative, as Lenin, Hitler, Georges Sorel, Gabriele D'Annunzio and Ayn Rand discovered.

The failure to tell a new story has been matched by an equally remarkable omission: the failure to discern and describe the values and principles that might inform our politics.

Know Your Values

Values are the bedrock of effective politics. They represent the importance we place on fundamental ways of being, offering a guide to what we consider to be good and worthwhile. They can often be described with single words.

For example, a person's dominant values may be wisdom, strength, honesty and freedom. This does not mean that these are the only values they hold, let alone that they always live by them, but that these are the aspirations they consider most important.

Our values tend to cluster around certain poles.[2] Social psychologists sometimes describe these poles as intrinsic and extrinsic. Intrinsic values, in their purest form, are expressed as compassion, connectedness and kindness towards all living beings, including oneself.[3] Extrinsic values are expressed as a desire for self-enhancement, through gaining, for example, status or power.

People with a strong set of intrinsic values and a weaker set of extrinsic values have high levels of self-acceptance, strong bonds of intimacy and a powerful desire to help other people. They are strongly inclined towards empathy, understanding, and independent thought and action. Research across seventy nations suggests that intrinsically motivated people are more open to change, have a stronger interest in universal rights and equality, and a stronger desire to protect and cherish both human beings and the natural world than more extrinsically motivated people.[4]

Most people, when asked what they care about, prioritise intrinsic values, placing community, friendship and equality at the top of the list.[5] Surveys of both children and adults reveal that the value which tends to be favoured above all others is what psychologists call 'benevolence', by which they mean protecting or advancing the welfare of people we know.[6]

The smaller number of people at the extrinsic end of the spectrum are more attracted to prestige, status, image, fame, power and wealth. They are strongly motivated by the prospect of individual reward and praise. They have little interest in cooperation or community. People who emphasise these values tend to report higher levels of stress, anxiety, anger, envy, dissatisfaction and depression than those at the intrinsic end.[7]

We are not born with these values. They are strongly shaped by our social environment, by the cues and responses we receive from other people, and by the stories we tell ourselves and each other. They are also shaped by the political environment.[8] If people live under a cruel and grasping political system, they tend to normalise and internalise it, absorbing its dominant trends and translating them into extrinsic values. This, in turn, permits an even crueller and more grasping political system to emerge.

If, by contrast, people live in a country in which no one is allowed to fall out of the boat, in which social norms are characterised by kindness, empathy, community and freedom from want and fear, their values are likely to shift towards the intrinsic end. This process is known as policy feedback, or the Values Ratchet.

Whether or not people become involved in civic life is influenced by their perceptions of their culture's dominant values. For example, research by the Common Cause Foundation reveals that if people perceive others to be mostly extrinsically motivated, they are less likely to vote in elections.[9]

When political parties dilute or abandon their values and adopt the values, phrases and stories of their opponents (a process known as triangulation), they change the political environment in which they operate. Like yeast in a barrel of beer, they generate the toxic conditions that eventually kill them.

If our purpose is to create a kinder world, we should embed within the political story we tell the intrinsic values that promote this aim: empathy, understanding, connectedness with other people, self-acceptance, independent thought and action.

Those who promote this story should know what their values are and be able to name them without hesitation or embarrassment. In doing so, they help to develop a social environment that fosters their aspirations, turning the Values Ratchet in the right direction. This is what many adherents of religion are able to do, and it might help to explain why some religions have survived for thousands of years.

Effective religious narratives, like effective political narratives, are often restoration stories. They tell us that, through the observance of faith and other religious values, we find redemption: the restoration of order in a broken world or a broken psyche.[10] The lesson religion has to teach politics is: first, know your values; then evangelise them in the form of powerful narratives.

Know Your Principles

Principles could be seen as the soil that derives from the bedrock of values. Political principles are the fundamental propositions at the heart of a political philosophy. In other words, they are a description of the world as we would like it to be. Again, they need to be expressed clearly and overtly, so that they can be explained and spread with pride and conviction.

With some politically engaged friends, I have drawn up a list of the principles that might help to inform a new political story.

A Statement of Principles

1. We want to live in a place guided by empathy, respect, justice, generosity, courage, fun and love.
2. We want to live in a place governed by judgements that

are honestly made, supported by evidence, accountable and transparent.

3. We want to live in a place in which everyone's needs are met, without harming the living world or the prosperity of future generations.

4. We want to live in a place in which the fruits of the work we do and the resources we use are fairly and widely distributed, in which shared prosperity is a general project, and the purpose of economic life is to enable universal well-being.

5. We want to live in a place in which all people have equal rights, in practice as well as in theory.

6. We want to live in a place in which all people can feel secure, confident, safe and cared for.

7. We want to live in a place in which, regardless of where they were born, everyone has a neighbourhood of which they feel proud, where they can freely participate in the life of the community.

8. We want to live in a place which, proudly and consistently, supports people in need of help, including those fleeing from danger and persecution abroad.

9. We want to live in a place in which a thriving natural world provides a refuge both for rich and abundant wildlife and for people seeking relief from the clamour of daily life.

10. We want to live in a place whose political system is fair and fully representative, in which everyone has a voice and every vote counts, and whose outcomes can neither be bought nor otherwise engineered.

11. We want to live in a place in which decisions are taken at the most appropriate level, to enhance democratic participation and connection.

12. We want to live in a place in which everyone has access to the information needed to make meaningful democratic choices, and in which political debate is honest, accessible and inclusive.

13. We want to live in a place in which education is a joyful process, encouraging children of all abilities to engage with enthusiasm, and adults to continue learning throughout their lives.

14. We want to live in a place in which good housing, fast and effective healthcare and a healthy, sufficient diet are available to everyone.

15. We want to live in a place that helps to build a safe, prosperous and resilient community of nations.

16. We want to live in a place that is open to new ideas and information, and that values creativity, research and discovery.

Attachment

A politics that has failed to articulate its values and principles leaves nothing to which people can attach themselves but policies. Policies should grow from the soil of principles. But, like the plants in our flowerbeds, they have a limited life. They must be replaced when circumstances change. If our only remaining attachments are to policies, we must break them when these policies are replaced. We are then asked to reattach ourselves to the new policies proposed by our favoured party or movement.

But attachment in politics is hard-won. Once broken, it tends to remain broken forever. Sustaining political momentum across years, decades, even generations, means developing and reinforcing lasting attachments. This means inducing political followers to love the soil – which, if carefully tended, lasts forever – rather than the plants that come and go.

In mainstream, inclusive politics today, the soil has been washed away. Parties have been growing their policies hydroponically.

A set of principles, important as it is, does not constitute a story. Nor can all the principles I have listed be incorporated into a story – they cover too much ground to create a coherent or satisfying narrative. But in seeking to develop one, we should be constantly aware of what we are trying to achieve. If the story succeeds, is it likely to advance these principles or clash with them? Is the political environment it creates likely to nurture the society they describe?

The Basics

The narrative we build, informed by our values and principles, has to be simple and intelligible. If it is to transform our politics, it should appeal to as many people as possible, crossing traditional party lines. It should resonate with deep needs and desires. It should explain the mess we are in and the means by which we might escape it. And, because there is nothing to be gained from spreading falsehoods, it must be firmly grounded in reality.

This might sound like a tall order, but there is, I believe, a clear and compelling story to be told that fits this description. First I will narrate it in detail, explaining the ideas and evidence that underpin it. Then I will summarise it in terms that are easy to grasp and remember.

The Story

Part 1: Original Virtue

There is something deeply weird about humanity. As an article in the journal *Frontiers in Psychology* points out, we are 'spectacularly unusual when compared to other animals'.[11] This phrase does not refer to our skills with language or our use of tools or ability to change our environment, remarkable though these are. It refers to our astonishing degree of altruism: our kindness towards other members of our species. We possess an unparalleled sensitivity to the needs of others, a unique level of concern about their welfare, and a peerless ability to create moral norms that generalise and enforce these tendencies.

Studies in neuroscience, psychology and evolutionary biology all point to the same conclusion: in this respect we are the extreme biological outlier.[12] Our astonishing tendencies emerge so early in our lives that they seem to be innate. In other words, we appear to have evolved to be this way. By the age of fourteen months, children begin to help each other, attempting to hand over objects another child cannot reach.[13] By the time they are two, they start sharing some of the things they value. By the age of three, they start to protest against other people's violations of moral norms.[14]

We are also, among mammals (with the possible exception of the naked mole rat),[15] the supreme cooperators. We evolved in the African savannahs: a world of fangs and claws and horns and tusks. We survived despite being weaker and slower than both our potential predators and most of our prey. We did so through developing, to an extraordinary degree, a capacity for mutual aid. As it was essential to our survival, this urge to cooperate was hard-wired into our brains through natural selection. It has not been lost.

Just as we feel physical pain to protect ourselves from physical injury, we feel emotional pain to protect ourselves from social injury. The emotional pain caused by isolation from other members of our group drove us to return to them, so that we did not get picked off by predators or die of starvation. Social pain and physical pain are processed in our brains by the same neural circuits (emotional pain, at some point in the evolution of social mammals, seems to have hijacked the physical pain network).[16] This might explain why, in many languages, it is hard to describe the impact of social dislocation without the words we use to denote physical pain and injury:[17] 'he broke my heart', 'I feel bruised by that argument', 'I was stung by her response', 'I'm hurting, real bad'.

Social contact reduces physical pain.[18] This is why we hug our children when they hurt themselves: affection is a powerful analgesic. Opioids relieve both physical agony and the distress of separation, which might explain the link between social isolation and drug addiction.[19]

Social pain can be harder to bear than physical pain, which could be why some people self-harm in response to emotional distress: it could be interpreted as an attempt to replace emotional injury with physical injury. As the prison system knows too well, one of the most effective forms of torture is solitary confinement.[20] We, the supremely social mammal, cannot cope alone: we need connection – togetherness – just as we need food and shelter.

Our extraordinary capacity for altruism and our remarkably social nature are the central, crucial facts about humankind. Yet we remain, to an astonishing degree, unaware of them. This is partly because our minds – which are always on the lookout for signs of danger – emphasise the rare but spectacular acts of violence a small proportion of the population inflicts on others, but not the daily acts of kindness and cooperation the rest of us perform, often unconsciously. This tendency is reinforced today by news reports.

We remember, for example, the two terrorists who murdered twelve people in Paris in January 2015, and our recollection of that horror persuades us that evil is a central feature of the human condition. Less prominent in our minds are the 3 million people in France and the millions elsewhere who gathered, lit candles and marched in public places in solidarity with the victims. These people, not the two terrorists, represent the human norm. Our innate tendency is to stand together against threats to our well-being, to treat an attack on one as an attack on all.

The reality such events obscure would make us gasp if we saw it in another species. Only because it is so familiar do we fail to notice that it is central to the human condition. Every day, I see people helping others with luggage, offering to cede their place in a queue, giving money to the homeless, setting aside time for others, listening to friends in distress, volunteering for causes which offer no material reward.

Occasionally we risk everything for the sake of other people – even for people we do not know. I think of my Dutch mother-in-law, whose family took in a six-year-old Jewish boy – a stranger – and hid him in their house for two years during the German occupation. The house next door was occupied by the local German commander; the street was often thick with soldiers and officials. Had the boy been discovered, the whole family would have been sent to a concentration camp, where they are likely to have been murdered.

This is what we are. But something has gone horribly wrong.

Part 2: Disorder

An epidemic of loneliness is sweeping the world. Once considered an affliction of older people, it is now tormenting people of other generations.[21] Our time is distinguished from previous eras by atomisation: the rupturing of social bonds, the collapse of shared ambitions and civic life, our unbearable isolation from each other. There are over 7 billion souls on Earth, but many people are unable to find anyone with whom they can connect.

The consequences are devastating. That loneliness (by which I mean the pain inflicted by involuntary isolation) causes unhappiness goes without saying. It is strongly associated with depression, paranoia, anxiety, insomnia, fear and the perception of threat.[22] It also has major impacts on our physical health, partly because it enhances production of the stress hormone cortisol, which suppresses the immune system. Chronic loneliness has been linked to dementia,[23] high blood pressure, heart disease and strokes,[24] lowered resistance to viruses[25] – even a higher rate of accidents. Some research suggests it has a comparable impact on physical health to smoking fifteen cigarettes a day,[26] and raises the risk of early death by 26 per cent.[27]

We live in an era of astonishing material wealth – albeit poorly distributed. But the great general advance in material conditions has not been accompanied, as our forebears might have expected, by general happiness. Instead, this age of atomisation breeds anxiety, discontent and dissatisfaction – conditions that afflict even the wealthiest classes.[28]

The intensity of this distress can be judged by the exotic means with which some people seek to address it: hiring 'people walkers',[29] designing robot partners, and procuring, for cash, 'friends' with whom we can pose for photographs that we can post on social media. In some countries, agencies rent out guests to underpopulated weddings. A recent article describes how, in Japan, one of these pretend guests was used to replace a sister with whom the bride had fallen out.[30] What, you might wonder, did the bride's mother make of it? She didn't seem to mind, probably because she had been hired as well.

Craving contentment and a sense of connection, we succumb to compulsions that often find expression in a frenzy of consumption. We chase brief spikes of satisfaction, which soon subside, to be replaced by the urge for another hit.

Consumerism – ever restless, never sated – threatens us with climate breakdown, helps catalyse a sixth great extinction, imperils global water supplies, and reduces the many wonders of the living world to the same grey waste. We rip the Earth's living systems apart to fill the gap in our lives, yet the gap remains. This compulsive, joyless hedonism consumes not only the wonders of nature, but also ourselves.

Loneliness is just one symptom of a wider crisis of alienation: a loss of connection with people and place, and with a sense of meaning and purpose. Society, the world's living systems, our happiness, our self-control, our sense of belonging: all are falling apart. Why has this happened?

Part 3: The Causes

Part of the answer is that this crisis is self-generating. The pursuit of material satisfactions dulls our concern for other people and for the living planet. It blinds us to our place in the world and the damage we impose on others. It propels us down a narrow corridor of self-interest, self-enhancement and immediate gratification.

These tendencies are reinforced by an economic system that puts a price on everything and a value on nothing; a political system that promotes economic growth above all other aims, regardless of whether it enhances human welfare or damages it; and organisational and technological changes that could scarcely have been better designed to drive us apart. We were once brought together by work, travel and entertainment. Now these activities tend to estrange us.

Globalisation has weakened our connections with our neighbours and neighbourhoods. Jobs are outsourced to cheaper workforces, causing, in some cases, the collapse of local economies and the communities that depended on them. Power is outsourced to global institutions we cannot influence, undermining our sense of self-ownership and political community. A globalised media creates the impression that, wherever we might be, life is elsewhere.

But above all, I believe, the trend towards social breakdown is driven by the dominant political narrative of our times. This narrative is a reiteration of the story told by the philosopher Thomas Hobbes in 1651. He asserted that the default state of human relations is a war of everyone against everyone else. Life in the state of nature, he famously observed, was 'solitary, poore, nasty, brutish, and short'.

It is not hard to see how he drew this conclusion, after witnessing the devastations of the English Civil War. His knowledge of human evolution was confined to the book of Genesis and informed by the doctrine of original sin. Today, knowing what we do about the nature and origins of humanity, we can state unequivocally that this view is mistaken. But it forms the text or subtext of much of the political thought and media commentary to which we are exposed.

Competition and individualism are the values at the heart of the twenty-first century's secular religion. Everywhere we are encouraged to fight for wealth and social position like stray dogs over a dustbin: competition, we are told, brutal as it may be, will enhance our lives to a greater extent than any other instrument. This story is supported by a rich mythology of rugged individualism, and advanced through an inspiring lexicon of lone rangers, sole traders, self-starters, self-made men and women, going it alone. The word 'people' has been widely replaced in the media by 'individuals'. The most cutting insult we can throw at someone is 'loser'.

Seeing some people grab vast wealth while others go hungry (at the time of writing, the world's eight richest people have the same net worth as the poorest half of its population)[31] reinforces the sense that this is a dog-eat-dog world. We either join the fight in the hope of triumphing over others or face destitution.

Many economists insist that we are typically selfish and self-maximising. They use a term to describe this perception of humanity that sounds serious and scientific: *Homo economicus*. Most of them seem to be unaware that the concept was formulated, by J. S. Mill and others, as a thought experiment. Soon it became a modelling tool. Then it became an ideal. Then it evolved into a description of who we really are.[32]

As a paper in a psychology journal observes,[33] *Homo economicus* is a reasonable description – of chimpanzees. 'Outsiders . . . would not expect to receive offers of food or solicitude; rather, they would be fiercely attacked', it notes of our closest living relatives. 'Food is shared only under harassment; even mothers will not voluntarily offer novel foods to their own infants unless the infants beg for them.' This, the paper notes, is an unreasonable description of human beings.

But we have heard the story of our competitive, self-maximising nature so often, and it is told with such panache and persuasive power, that we have accepted it as an account of who we really are. It has changed our perception of ourselves. Our perceptions, in turn, change the way we behave.

Part 4: The Consequences
One result of this mistaken belief is the loss of common purpose. Our tendency is to stop seeing ourselves as people striving together to overcome our common problems, and to view ourselves instead as people striving against each other to overcome our individual problems. Never mind that these problems are often much bigger than we are, and arise from structural forces that no person acting alone can tackle. As

individualism is the religion of our times, it must be the solution to whatever crisis we face.

Everywhere we seem to hear the same low, insistent whisper: 'You are on your own.' Neither the state nor society will save us. They will not solve our problems, even if these problems – such as climate change or economic crises or public health disasters – cannot be addressed by other means. No solutions are proposed for insecurity, precarity and desperation. Indeed, as the cruel eighteenth-century doctrines of Thomas Malthus and Joseph Townsend – 'it is only hunger which can spur and goad them on to labour' – are disinterred, precarity and desperation are recast as the necessary incentives to encourage the poor to work harder.[34]

The loss of common purpose leads in turn to a loss of belief in ourselves as a force for change. Many, in recent years, lost their belief in the promise of democracy: that, through voting, mobilising and campaigning, we can make our political systems work for all of us, rather than just a select few. We have tended to face our crises with passivity and resignation.

Faith in democratic norms is collapsing. A study published in the *Journal of Democracy* revealed that, while 72 per cent of those born before the Second World War in the United States believed it was essential to live in a democracy, this figure fell to just 30 per cent of those born in 1980.[35] One in six of the people surveyed asserted that army rule would be a good or very good development – a proportion that has more than doubled in twenty years. A similar slump in political faith has taken place in other countries.

If politics as usual no longer delivers, people look elsewhere for answers. This 'elsewhere' often means demagoguery:

movements characterised by the extreme simplification of political choices, the abandonment of reasoned argument, and scapegoating. The reaction against democratic failure has licensed a clutch of suppressed hatreds – of women, immigrants, racial and religious minorities, difference of all kinds. We witness the resurgence of the kind of politics that until recently seemed to be everywhere in retreat.

The potential consequences are grave. Governments founded on lies and exaggerations are making promises they cannot possibly keep, and blaming an ever wider array of scapegoats when they fail to materialise. If jobs are destroyed en masse by automation, this will enhance the need for distraction. As people become angrier and more alienated, the net of blame will be cast wider.

Eventually the anger that cannot be answered through policy will be turned outwards, towards other nations. Lacking other means of disguising their failures or establishing legitimacy, governments will discover the potential of foreign aggression. Terrorism provides ample opportunities for justification. Major war, which seemed until recently a distant prospect, begins to look like a plausible threat.

Part 5: Restoration

We are better than we are told we are, better than we are induced to be. By recognising our good nature and coming together to express it, we can overcome the multiple crises we face that cannot be solved alone. By reconnecting with each other we can conquer loneliness, unhappiness and the loss of our sense of meaning and purpose.

Though we still need it, we can no longer rely only on the state. Nor can we rely on the workplace to supply either social connection or economic security. But we can find some of the help we seek in community. By reviving community, built around the places in which we live, and by anchoring ourselves, our politics and parts of our economy in the life of this community, we can recover the best aspects of our humanity. We can mobilise our remarkable nature for our own good and the good of our neighbours.

We will no longer walk alone. We will no longer work alone. We will no longer feel alone. We will restore our sense of belonging: belonging to ourselves, belonging to our communities, belonging to our localities, belonging to the world. In turn, we will develop a politics and an economy that belong to us. By rebuilding community, we will renew democracy and the hope we invest in it. We will develop political systems that are not so big that they cannot respond to us but not so small that they cannot meet the problems we face. We will achieve something that, paradoxically, we cannot realise alone: self-reliance. By helping each other, we help ourselves.

The strong, embedded cultures we develop will be robust enough to accommodate social diversity of all kinds: a diversity of people, of origins, of life experiences, of ideas and ways of living. We will no longer need to fear people who differ from ourselves; we will have the strength and confidence to reject attempts to channel hatred towards them.

By rebuilding community, we become proud of our society, proud of our institutions, proud of our nations, proud of ourselves. By coming together we discover who we are. We ignite our capacity for empathy and altruism. Togetherness and belonging allow us to become the heroes of the story.

The Story – in Summary

We are astonishing creatures, blessed with an amazing capacity for kindness and care towards others. But this good nature has been thwarted by a mistaken view of our own humanity. We have been induced by certain politicians, economists and commentators to accept a vicious ideology of extreme competition and individualism that pits us against each other, encourages us to fear and mistrust each other, and weakens the social bonds that make our lives worth living.

Though it is not the only factor, this has helped to usher in an age of loneliness, in which, on this crowded planet, we are disconnected from each other as never before. The result is an epidemic of unhappiness and of psychological and physical illness. The atomisation we suffer has eroded our sense of common purpose and sapped our belief that, by working together, we can change life for the better. It has undermined democracy, and allowed intolerant and violent forces to fill the political vacuum. We are trapped in a vicious circle of alienation and reaction.

By coming together to revive community life, we, the heroes of this story, can break the vicious circle. Through invoking the two great healing forces – togetherness and belonging – we can rediscover the central facts of our humanity: our altruism and mutual aid.

Where there is atomisation, we will create a thriving civic life. Where there is alienation, we will forge a new sense of belonging: to neighbours, neighbourhood and society. Where we find ourselves crushed between market and state, we will develop a new economics that treats both people and planet with respect. Where we are ignored and exploited, we will revive democracy and retrieve politics from those who have captured it.

In doing so, we can reclaim our happiness, reclaim our self-reliance, reclaim our pride, and reclaim our place. We will belong once more both to society and to ourselves.

I propose a name for this story: 'The Politics of Belonging'.

Speaking to Everyone

Though I do not seek to disguise my own inclinations, my aim is to reach anyone to whom a generous, inclusive politics might appeal. I hope that the story I have told has the potential to speak to people of all denominations.

Community, togetherness and belonging are values invoked across the political spectrum. Thomas Paine and Edmund Burke might have agreed on little else, but in this respect they seemed to be as one. Paine wrote: 'The mutual dependence and reciprocal interest which man has upon man, and all the parts of civilised community upon each other, create that great chain of connection which holds it together.'[36] Burke famously insisted: 'To be attached to the subdivision, to love the little platoon we belong to in society, is the first principle (the germ as it were) of public affections. It is the first link in the series by which we proceed towards a love to our country, and to mankind.'[37] Few people would disagree with either writer on this point.

Many of those who have voted for demagogues and extremists have stumbled into this choice through disillusionment, alienation and the absence of stories that make sense of their lives. Most are not ill-intentioned. When they heard someone calling through the political void – someone who, instead of speaking in robotic platitudes, named their problems and promised solutions, however crude and unlikely those solutions were – they responded. A few years previously, they might have voted for parties that emphasised entirely different values.

Perhaps, in these fluid and fissiparous times, almost everyone should now be seen as a swing voter. The task of effective politics today is to reach across the divides and find common ground, however unlikely this might at first appear. I believe that the themes I explore in this chapter have this potential.

Extending the Story

I have sketched out the basic components of a new story. But if it is to help to catalyse change, we need to know more. We need a deeper understanding of the problems we confront. Chapters 2 and 3 seek to explain in more detail how the multiple crises we face developed, and how the failure to produce a new narrative has allowed these crises to persist. Chapter 4 then shows how these crises translate into alienation, and how this then spawns a series of new political crises.

Then I come to the central task of this book, which is to show how community can be rebuilt and how the politics of belonging might develop. With the help of an excellent researcher, Charlie Young, I have sought feasible examples of the policies and practices through which this story can be told. These are explored in chapters 5, 6, 7 and 8. Our survey is by no means comprehensive, and new ideas and inspiring examples are emerging all the time, but I hope to have supplied a broad impression of what can be done. Chapter 9 explores the strategies and tactics through which these policies might be implemented, and Chapter 10 offers a brief description of the point this process has reached, and what the next steps may be.

I see this book as just one of the many building blocks required to construct a new politics. It sits upon the foundational work of many inspiring people, and I hope it will encourage others to contribute to a new political architecture. Like all the best things in life, this is something we should build together.

2

A Captive Audience

The belief that competition and individualism are humanity's defining features did not arise spontaneously. Though it has a long heritage, it was refined in the twentieth century by the most powerful political narrative in circulation today: the story told by neoliberalism. This ideology continues to dominate our political and economic systems, and almost every aspect of our lives.

Neoliberalism has seeped into our language, our understanding of the choices we face and our conception of ourselves. For this reason, it has become almost invisible to us: we cannot step back far enough to see it. Even the name, which was coined by those who first told this story, has been disowned and buried.

In Chapter 1, I briefly described neoliberalism's narrative outline. But to understand why we are trapped in a mistaken view of ourselves, and how it affects the choices we make, we need to know more about what the doctrine is, how and why it arose, and why it persists.

Human Capital

Neoliberalism, like many successful political narratives, provides not only a set of economic or political ideas, but also an account of who we are and how we behave. It defines us as competitors, guided above all other impulses by the urge to get ahead of our fellows. This urge, it argues, should be cultivated and encouraged. Our democratic choices are best exercised by buying and selling – a process that automatically rewards merit and punishes inefficiency. By discovering a natural hierarchy of winners and losers, 'the market' creates a more efficient system than could ever be devised through planning or design.

Defined by the market, defined as a market, human society should be run in every respect as if it were a business, its social relations reimagined as commercial transactions; people redesignated as human capital. The aim and purpose of society is to maximise profits.

Attempts to limit competition are treated as hostile to liberty. Tax and regulation should be minimised; public services should be privatised or reconstructed in the image of the market. The organisation of labour and collective bargaining by trade unions are portrayed as market distortions that prevent the natural winners and losers from being discovered. Inequality is recast as virtuous: a reward for usefulness and a generator of wealth, which trickles down to enrich everyone. Efforts to create a more equal society are both counterproductive and morally corrosive.

So pervasive has neoliberalism become that we seldom even recognise it as an ideology. We appear to accept the proposition that this utopian faith describes a neutral force

– a kind of biological law, like Darwin's theory of evolution. But the philosophy arose as a conscious attempt to reshape human life and shift the locus of power.

A Heroic Narrative

The term neoliberalism was invented at a meeting in Paris in 1938.[1] Among the delegates were two men who came to define the ideology, Ludwig von Mises and Friedrich Hayek. Both exiles from Austria, they saw social democracy, exemplified by Franklin Roosevelt's New Deal and the gradual development of Britain's welfare state, as examples of a collectivism that occupied the same spectrum as Nazism and communism.

In *The Road to Serfdom*, published in 1944, Hayek argued that government planning, by crushing individualism, would lead inexorably to totalitarian control.[2] Partly as a result of people's justifiable fear of the state power marshalled and deployed by both fascism and Soviet communism, his book influenced a wide range of readers. Among them were some of the world's wealthiest people, who were chafing against restraints imposed by the state, such as high taxes and strong public protections. They saw in the story he told an opportunity to challenge the prevailing political narrative of the time: the narrative of social democracy. When, in 1947, Hayek and others founded the first organisation that would spread the doctrine of neoliberalism – the Mont Pelerin Society – it was supported financially by millionaires and their foundations.[3]

With their help, Friedrich Hayek began to create a transatlantic network of academics, businessmen, journalists and activists. The movement's rich backers funded a series of think tanks that would refine and promote the ideology. Among them were the American Enterprise Institute, the Heritage Foundation, the Cato Institute, the Institute of Economic Affairs, the Centre for Policy Studies and the Adam Smith Institute.[4] They also financed academic positions and departments, particularly at the universities of Chicago and Virginia.

As it evolved, neoliberalism became more strident. By the time he wrote *The Constitution of Liberty*, published in 1960,[5] Hayek had come to reject such notions as political freedom, universal rights, human equality and the redistribution of wealth. All these, he argued, by restricting the freedoms of the rich and powerful, intrude on the creation of wealth, thereby causing harm to others. The freedoms of the opulent, he contended, should be absolute. Democracy, by contrast, 'is not an ultimate or absolute value'. In fact, liberty depends on preventing the majority from exercising choice over the direction that politics and society might take.

He justified this position by creating a heroic narrative of extreme wealth. He conflated the economic elite, spending their money in new ways, with philosophical and scientific pioneers. Just as the political philosopher should be free to think the unthinkable, so the very rich should be free to do the undoable, without constraint by public interest or public opinion.

The ultra-rich are 'scouts', 'experimenting with new styles of living', who blaze the trails that the rest of society will follow. The progress of society depends on the liberty of these 'independents' to gain as much money as they want and spend it how they wish. All that is good and useful, therefore, arises from inequality. There should be no connection between merit and reward, no distinction made between earned and unearned income, and no limit to the rent that can be charged.

Inherited wealth, he claimed, is more socially useful than earned wealth: 'the idle rich', who don't have to work for their money, can devote themselves to influencing 'fields of thought and opinion, of tastes and beliefs'. Even when they seem to be spending money on nothing but 'aimless display', they are in fact acting as society's vanguard.

Hayek softened his opposition to monopolies and hardened his opposition to trade unions. He lambasted progressive taxation and attempts by the state to raise the general welfare of citizens. He railed against free universal healthcare and dismissed the conservation of natural resources.

Outbreak

At first, despite its lavish funding, neoliberalism remained at the margins. The postwar consensus was almost universal: John Maynard Keynes's economic prescriptions were widely applied; full employment and the relief of poverty were common goals in the United States and much of western Europe; top rates of tax were high; and governments sought social outcomes without embarrassment, developing new public services and safety nets.

But in the 1970s, when Keynesian policies began to fall apart and economic crises struck on both sides of the Atlantic, neoliberal ideas entered the mainstream. As Milton Friedman, the most influential neoliberal in the United States, remarked, 'when the time came that you had to change . . . there was an alternative ready there to be picked up'.[6] With the help of sympathetic journalists and political advisers,[7] elements of neoliberalism, especially its prescriptions for monetary policy, were adopted by Jimmy Carter's administration in the United States and Jim Callaghan's government in Britain.

According to party folklore, in 1975, a few months after Margaret Thatcher became leader of the Conservatives in the United Kingdom, she was chairing a meeting at which one of her colleagues explained what he saw as the core beliefs of Conservatism. She snapped open her handbag, pulled out a dog-eared copy of *The Constitution of Liberty*, and slammed it on the table. '*This* is what we believe', she said.[8] A political revolution had begun that would sweep the world.

When she took office in 1979, she sought to apply Hayek's doctrines to the letter: massive tax cuts for the rich, the crushing of trade unions, deregulation, privatisation, outsourcing and competition in public services. Recently released documents reveal that she tried to go the whole way, dismantling the welfare state, shutting down free universal healthcare and charging fees for education.[9] But she was prevented from completing the programme by her own party.

Ronald Reagan, who assumed the US presidency in 1980, followed the same prescriptions. The overarching aim was to destroy the collective bargaining power of workers, removing the primary source of resistance to the power of Hayek's 'independents'. Hayek's story gave Thatcher and Reagan the focus required to generate long-term change.

Through the IMF, the World Bank, the Maastricht Treaty and the World Trade Organisation, neoliberal policies were imposed – often without democratic consent – on much of the world. Most remarkable was the ideology's adoption by parties that once belonged to the left, such as Labour in the UK and the Democrats in the United States (I explore their failures in the following chapter).

Reproduction

It was not only among political parties that the doctrine spread. We have all internalised and reproduced its creeds. The rich persuade themselves that they acquired their wealth through merit, ignoring the advantages – such as education, inheritance and class – that may have helped to secure it. The poor begin to blame themselves for their failures, even when they can do little to change their circumstances.

If you do not have a job, the relentless whisper tells you, it is not because of structural unemployment, but because you are unenterprising. If your credit card is maxed out, it is not because of the impossible costs of housing but because you are feckless and improvident. If your children are unfit, it is not because their school has sold its playing field but because you are a bad parent. In a world governed by competition, those who fall behind come to be defined and self-defined as losers. The rich are the new righteous, while the poor are the new deviants, who have failed both economically and morally, and are now classified as social parasites.

These shifts correlate with a sharp rise in certain psychiatric conditions in countries such as the United States and United Kingdom: self-harm, eating disorders, depression and personality disorders.[10] Performance anxiety and social phobia spread like fungus. They reflect a fear of other people, who are perceived as both evaluators and competitors: among the few remaining social roles neoliberalism envisages.

Not only have we adopted the words neoliberalism uses; we have accepted its definitions. 'The market' sounds like a natural system that might bear upon us equally, like gravity or atmospheric pressure. But it is fraught with power relations. What 'the market wants' tends to mean what corporations and their bosses want.

As Andrew Sayer points out in *Why We Can't Afford the Rich*, 'investment' means two quite different things.[11] One is the funding of productive and socially useful activities, the other is the purchase of existing assets to milk them for rent, interest, dividends and capital gains. Using the same word for different activities 'camouflages the sources of wealth', leading us to confuse wealth extraction with wealth creation.

Rentiers and inheritors now style themselves 'entrepreneurs' or 'wealth creators', claiming to have earned their unearned income. This is a perfect reversal of the way in which the rich sought social acceptance a century ago, when entrepreneurs – disparaged as nouveaux riches, parvenus, bounders and social climbers – tried to pass themselves off as rentiers.

Freedom for the Pike

It may seem strange that a doctrine promising choice and freedom should have been promoted with Mrs Thatcher's slogan: 'There is no alternative'. But, as Hayek remarked on a visit to Pinochet's Chile – one of the first nations in which the programme was comprehensively applied – 'my personal preference leans toward a liberal dictatorship rather than toward a democratic government devoid of liberalism'.[12] The freedom that neoliberalism offers, which sounds so beguiling when expressed in general terms, turns out to mean freedom for the pike, not for the minnows.[13]

Freedom from trade unions and collective bargaining means the freedom to suppress wages. Freedom from regulation means the freedom to poison rivers, endanger workers, charge iniquitous rates of interest and design exotic financial instruments. Freedom from tax means freedom from the distribution of wealth that binds society together.

Another paradox of neoliberalism is that universal competition relies upon universal quantification and comparison. The result is that workers, job-seekers and public services of every kind are subject to a pettifogging, infantilising regime of surveillance and auditing, designed to identify the winners and punish the losers. The doctrine that Ludwig Von Mises proposed would free us from the bureaucratic nightmare of central planning[14] has instead created one.

But it works, spectacularly, for some. Economic growth has been markedly slower in the neoliberal era (since 1980 in Britain and the United States) than it was in the preceding decades; but not for the wealthiest.[15] Inequality in the distribution of both income and wealth, after sixty years of decline, rose rapidly in this period, due to the breaking of trade unions, tax reductions, rising rents, privatisation and deregulation.[16]

The privatisation or marketisation of public services such as energy, water, trains, health, education, roads and prisons has enabled corporations to set up tollbooths in front of essential assets and charge rent, either to citizens or to government, for their use. Rent is another term for unearned income. When you pay an inflated price for a train ticket, only part of the fare compensates the operators for the money they spend on fuel, wages, rolling stock and other outlays. The rest reflects the fact that you have no choice but to pay.[17]

Those who own and run privatised or semi-privatised public services make stupendous fortunes by investing little and charging much. In Russia and India, oligarchs acquired state assets through fire-sales. In Mexico, Carlos Slim was granted control of almost all landline and mobile phone services, and soon became the world's richest man.

Financialisation has had a similar impact, enhancing the opportunities for the rich to acquire unearned income, in this case through interest payments. These, in aggregate, amount to a transfer of money from the poor to the rich. As property prices and the withdrawal of state funding load people with debt, the banks and their executives clean up.

Manifest Failure

Neoliberal policies are everywhere beset by ideological failure. Not only are the banks too big to fail, but so are the corporations now charged with delivering public services. Even in the most debased democracies, vital services cannot be allowed to collapse. The state must intervene to support them when disaster threatens.[18] Business takes the profits, the state keeps the risk.

Perhaps the most dangerous impact of neoliberalism is not the economic crises it has caused, but the political crises. As the domain of the state is reduced, our ability to change the course of our lives through voting also contracts. Instead, neoliberal theory asserts, people can exercise choice through spending. But some have more to spend than others: in the great consumer or shareholder democracy, votes are not equally distributed. The result is a disempowerment of the poor and middle. As parties across the political spectrum adopt similar neoliberal policies, disempowerment turns to disenfranchisement.

If their dominant ideology stops governments from changing social outcomes and delivering social justice, they can no longer respond to the needs of the electorate. Politics becomes irrelevant to people's lives; debate is reduced to the yabber of a remote elite. The disenfranchised turn instead to a virulent anti-politics, in which facts and arguments are replaced by slogans, symbols and sensation.[19]

The paradoxical result is that the backlash against neoliberalism's crushing of political choice elevates the kind of people Hayek worshipped. Donald Trump, who won the US presidency despite – or because of – his failure to articulate a coherent set of policies, is not a classic neoliberal. But he is the perfect representation of Hayek's 'independent': the beneficiary of inherited wealth, unconstrained by common morality, whose gross predilections strike a new path that others may follow.

Invisible Doctrine

The most remarkable aspect of neoliberalism is that it is still here. Its evident and devastating failures have not dislodged it. When the system it built came crashing down, the ideology survived. If anything, it has become more extreme. Governments have used neoliberal crises as both excuse and opportunity to cut taxes, privatise remaining public services, rip holes in the social safety net, deregulate corporations and re-regulate citizens. The self-hating state now sinks its teeth into every organ of the public sector.

There are two principal reasons for this astonishing feat of survival. The first is that, as a result of its anonymity, we have failed until recently even to recognise neoliberalism as a system of thought, let alone as the ideology responsible for many of the crises we face. Instead, in common with other all-pervasive systems, we have seen it as nothing more than the natural order of things.

Those who promote neoliberalism have gone to some lengths to keep its mechanics hidden from view. The invisible doctrine of the invisible hand is promoted by invisible backers. The Institute of Economic Affairs, which has argued forcefully and repeatedly in the media against the further regulation of the tobacco industry, has been secretly funded by British American Tobacco since 1963.[20] Charles and David Koch, two of the richest men in the world, founded the institute – Americans for Prosperity – that set up the Tea Party movement.[21] Charles Koch, in establishing one of his think tanks, noted that 'in order to avoid undesirable criticism, how the organization is controlled and directed should not be widely advertised'.[22]

We cannot contest a narrative until we have named it.

Proving Thatcher Right

The second reason for neoliberalism's remarkable longevity is the absence of countervailing stories. When laissez-faire economics led to catastrophe in 1929, John Maynard Keynes devised a comprehensive economic theory to replace it, supported by a powerful narrative of restoration and redemption. When Keynesian demand management hit the buffers in the 1970s, there was an alternative ready: neoliberalism. But when neoliberalism fell apart in 2008, the political parties appeared to vindicate Margaret Thatcher's maxim: there was, indeed, no alternative.

Governing and major opposition parties responded to the crises caused by neoliberalism in three ways. Some sought to strengthen and extend the doctrine. Some sought to soften it, offering a milder version of the thinking that got us into this mess. Others made a pilgrimage to the grave of Lord Keynes, disinterred his body and tried to pump it back to life.

All these parties were exposed by the Great Crash as empty – bereft of the unifying narratives on which political movements depend. Across the thirty years of the neoliberal era, they had failed to produce a new story, or even to recognise the need for one. This failure, in its scale and impacts, matches the failures of neoliberalism. It helps to explain the implosion of mainstream political parties across the world.

It was not enough to oppose a broken system. Neither was it enough to appease it. A coherent alternative was required, and no such thing had been prepared. For all its flaws and failures, we can learn from neoliberalism the most important political lesson of all. To change the world, you must tell a story: a story of hope and transformation that tells us who we are.

3

Don't Look Back

The political history of the second half of the twentieth century could be summarised as the conflict between its two great narratives: neoliberalism and social democracy. Social democracy in this era, whose story I briefly summarised in Chapter 1, acquired much of its power and coherence from the thinking of one remarkable man.

Across four decades, John Maynard Keynes's work dominated economic thought and practice. During the period the French call the *trente glorieuses* – 1945 to 1975 – his prescriptions are widely credited with reviving economies and distributing their benefits. That they remain more or less the only mainstream alternative to neoliberalism today reveals a remarkable stagnation of both thought and ambition.

Tell Me the Old, Old Story

The first and most obvious problem with an attempt to use Keynesian social democracy as a core political narrative is that (if we date his ideological dominance from the *General Theory of Employment, Interest and Money*, published in 1936)[1] the story is more than eighty years old. Political stories need to be renewed. If politics does not feel fresh, it struggles to kindle the imaginative excitement from which hope arises.

The second problem is that the surviving enthusiasm for Keynes among mainstream parties is highly selective. It has been reduced in most cases to lowering interest rates when economies are sluggish and engaging in tepid counter-cyclical public spending: which means injecting public money into the economy when unemployment is high or recession threatens. Other Keynesian measures, such as raising taxes when an economy grows quickly, to dampen the boom-bust cycle; the fixed exchange rate system; capital controls and a self-balancing global banking system (an International Clearing Union) – all of which Keynes saw as essential complements to these policies – have been discarded and forgotten.

Not only does this ensure that the rich old story has been reduced to two thin chapters, whose loss of context destroys their narrative power; but the absence of other Keynesian measures (as well as changed global circumstances) weakens the effectiveness of the remaining elements of policy. Let me give you an example.

In 2009, in the hope of boosting the economy in the wake of the financial crash, the British government spent £300 million on stimulating sales of new cars.[2] Under its scrappage scheme, if car owners traded in their old vehicles for new ones, the government, with the help of manufacturers, knocked £2,000 off the price. This lavish programme was partly justified as an environmental measure, though it was clear from the outset that it would lead to a rise in environmental impacts, as the materials and energy used in manufacturing new cars outweighed any likely savings from better fuel economy. Its primary purpose was to boost British car assembly plants and protect the jobs of their workers.

But European state aid rules forbade such schemes from discriminating between cars made in Britain and cars made abroad. British car plants assembled only some 15 per cent of the vehicles sold in the country,[3] which meant that 85 per cent of the benefit went to car plants in Germany, Japan and other manufacturing nations. We could see this spending as foreign aid – to some of the world's richest nations.

The current pattern of globalisation, which developed partly as a result of abandoning the fixed exchange rates and capital controls Keynes advocated, ensures that this problem is to some extent repeated wherever Keynesian stimulus spending is applied. It might lead to a general (if scarcely detectable) global economic uplift, but the domestic impact will necessarily be weaker than Keynes intended.

This issue is compounded by the phenomenon of job-free growth, caused in part by the automation now spreading into almost every economic sector. Today, governments pull the starter cord – spending public money and cutting interest rates – that ignited employment in the past, only to discover that it snaps before the motor fires. Two feeble measures, removed from the rich framework of thought and narrative in which they were once embedded, have little chance of sustaining a political revival.

Capital Strike

Another issue is that the troubles that beset the Keynesian model in the 1970s have not disappeared. While the oil embargo in 1973 was the immediate trigger for the lethal combination of high inflation and high unemployment ('stagflation') that Keynesian policies were almost powerless to counteract, problems with the system had been mounting for years. Falling productivity and rising cost-push inflation (wages and prices pursuing each other upwards) were already beginning to erode support for Keynesian economics. Most importantly, perhaps, the programme had buckled in response to the political demands of capital.

Strong financial regulations and controls on the movement of money began to weaken in the 1950s, as governments started to liberalise financial markets.[4] Richard Nixon's decision in 1971 to suspend the convertibility of dollars into gold destroyed the system of fixed exchange rates on which much of the success of Keynes's policies depended. The capital controls introduced to prevent financiers and speculators from sucking money out of balanced, Keynesian economies collapsed. Today, it is hard to find a mainstream politician in Europe or the Anglophone nations – including those who call themselves Keynesians – prepared to call for their reintroduction.

We cannot hope that the strategies deployed by global finance that helped to destroy the efficacy of Keynes's measures in the 1970s will be unlearned. If the soft Keynesianism proposed by opponents of neoliberalism is to amount to anything but tinkering, it has to confront a wider set of challenges than most of its advocates have yet been prepared to acknowledge.

But perhaps the biggest problem residual Keynesianism confronts in the twenty-first century is that, when it does work, it collides headfirst with the environmental crisis. A programme that seeks to sustain employment through constant economic growth driven by consumer demand seems destined to exacerbate our greatest predicament. The intensity of energy and resource use (in other words, the amount used for every unit of economic activity) might decline, but in most cases the overall volume of fuel and materials consumed continues to rise as growth outstrips efficiency improvements.[5] In its current incarnation, at any rate, economic growth appears incompatible with the protection of the living planet. This is another way of saying it is incompatible with the continued prosperity of humankind.

While certain Keynesian prescriptions (such as the spend-ing governments deployed to prevent the 2008 financial crisis from spiralling into economic collapse) remain available and useful, it is not easy to see how a return to Keynesianism as a central doctrine can work politically, economically or ecologically. It provides neither a coherent answer to the multiple crises we face nor the compelling new story that might inspire political revival.

Bermuda Triangulation

Without a new, guiding story of their own, allowing them to look towards a better future rather than a better past, it was inevitable that political parties which once sought to resist the power of corporations and the very rich would lose their sense of direction. They appeared to believe they could prosper by becoming as mute and inoffensive as possible. The result was retreat, confusion and betrayal.

In the neoliberal era, the principal strategy of the leaders of these parties, such as Bill Clinton and Tony Blair, was to triangulate.[6] This means that they extracted a few elements of what their parties had once believed, mixed them with elements of what their opponents believed, and developed from this unlikely combination a 'third way'. It was inevitable that the blazing, insurrectionary confidence of neoliberalism would exert a stronger gravitational pull than the dying star of social democracy.

For the first time in over a century of Democratic policy, Bill Clinton's first platform (his manifesto) made no mention of controlling corporate monopolies. Through mergers and acquisitions, monopoly power burgeoned during his presidency. He deregulated the financial sector (through the repeal of the Glass–Steagall Act), licensing the recklessness that led to the financial crisis of 2008. He allowed Alan Greenspan, chair of the Federal Reserve, to apply the doctrines of Friedrich Hayek and Milton Friedman rigidly to monetary policy.

He completed the ratification of NAFTA – the North American Free Trade Agreement – which permitted corporations to acquire legal powers over democratic assemblies. He pressed world trade bodies to expand the definition and scope of intellectual property, allowing corporations to enclose what had previously belonged to everyone and no one. Bill and Hillary Clinton found new donors among the exceedingly rich, particularly on Wall Street.[7]

Their party had already moved a long way from the days when Woodrow Wilson promised to 'destroy the trusts', or Franklin Roosevelt told Congress that 'the liberty of a democracy is not safe if the people tolerate the growth of private power to a point where it becomes stronger than their democratic state itself'.[8] Under Clinton, the party appeared to forget the warning by the Supreme Court judge and stalwart of the Democrats in the first half of the twentieth century, Louis Brandeis: 'We may have democracy, or we may have wealth concentrated in the hands of a few, but we can't have both.'[9]

The influx of corporate money and corporate thinking dramatically curtailed the party's capacity to change social outcomes. The remnants of the vigorous programmes of legislation and taxation pursued by Franklin Roosevelt and Harry Truman, which confronted inequality and protected the American people from patrimonial power, were – sometimes actively, mostly passively – abandoned or reversed under Bill Clinton. They became lost in his Bermuda triangulation.

The Mendacity of Hope

The hope that Barack Obama inspired was not fulfilled. Instead of using the aftermath of the 2008 financial crash as an opportunity to restrain corporate and financial power, he sought to reinstate it. He bailed out the banks, but he left the victims of foreclosure (the repossession of homes from people who have not been able to maintain their mortgage payments) to fend for themselves. Though the sub-prime mortgage lending that caused the foreclosure crisis was driven by irresponsible and often fraudulent practices, the full cost fell on the debtors, while the reckless creditors were protected.

Mass foreclosure was not an accident of policy, according to testimony by Obama's Treasury secretary, Timothy Geithner; it was the policy. Allowing up to 10 million foreclosures, he said, would 'help foam the runway' for the banks (this refers to the practice of covering runways with fire-suppressant foam when aircraft need to make an emergency landing).[10] The aim was to protect the banks at all costs: impoverished homeowners were seen as the necessary sacrifice. There could scarcely have been a more powerful symbol of abandonment, of both people and values.

The Justice Department and the attorney general failed to pursue what appeared to be clear instances of criminal wrongdoing on the part of financiers. This reinforced the corrosive sense that, as a result of its political power, Wall Street enjoys effective legal impunity. Obama's policy on monopolies fell somewhere between the feeble and the nonexistent, with the result that economic power was further concentrated. During the first three years of his presidency, an astonishing 95 per cent of the income growth in the United States was captured by the richest 1 per cent of earners.[11]

Obama pressed for trade agreements that appeared to have less to do with bringing down tariff barriers than with transferring economic and political power from citizens to corporations, such as the Trans-Pacific Partnership, the Transatlantic Trade and Investment Partnership (TTIP) and the Trade in Services Agreement.

The extent to which he was insulated – either by his advisers or by his belief system – from public opinion became apparent when he visited Britain to advise its people to stay in the European Union. If they left the EU, he warned, the UK would be 'in the back of the queue'[12] for a new trade agreement with the United States. Given that the agreement the European Union was trying to negotiate with the United States (the deeply unpopular TTIP) was one of the forces driving people towards Brexit, his threat sounded more like a promise.

The result of the Democratic Party's many contracts with elite power was that large numbers of Americans, without representatives who were prepared to defend or even recognise their interests, abandoned politics, aware that it had abandoned them. In the mid-term congressional elections of 2014, turnout fell to 36 per cent[13] – the lowest level since 1942, when many voters were otherwise engaged overseas.

Nothing was learned. Leaked emails from Hillary Clinton's campaign for the 2016 presidency revealed a pattern of demeaning transactions with major funders.[14] These people – among the richest in America – were flattered and cultivated at every turn. They were allowed to set the limits of the party's ambitions – limits that help to account for Clinton's failure to inspire potential voters. The Democratic Party's grovelling ensured that the very rich owned both halves of the presidential contest.

The Longest Till Receipt in History

In 2015, the British Labour Party fought a general election it was widely expected to win (if not with an absolute majority). But its manifesto looked more like a giant till receipt than a political programme.[15] It was fully costed, funded, ordered and itemised, but lacked any sense of optimism, proposition or purpose.

Those who drafted it had taken great pains to assure the billionaire press that they presented no threat, but neglected to assure the voters that they offered anything worth voting for. They meekly echoed the Conservative party's agenda of corporation tax cuts, social security caps and austerity. They accepted and reproduced the government's claim (which has since all but vanished from political life) that reducing the deficit should be the foremost aim of contemporary politics.

The centrepiece of Labour's manifesto was its 'budget responsibility lock' – a promise to keep faith with the Conservative doctrine of forswearing all additional borrowing, regardless of economic circumstance or public need. It should not be surprising that a party offering a modified version of its opponents' policies lost the election: if people want the real thing, they vote for it; if no alternative is on offer, they do not vote at all. And, if the opportunity arises, they express their disgust at this general failure to inspire or excite by aiming a kick at the entire political establishment, which is one explanation for the vote to leave the European Union.

The Great Surprise

In April 2017, the Conservative Prime Minister, Theresa May, unexpectedly called a general election, confident of a crushing victory. At the time, an opinion poll put support for the Conservatives at 48 per cent, while Labour stood at 24 per cent.[16] Local elections, held two weeks after her announcement (and just five weeks before the general election), seemed to confirm this expectation. Labour was trounced, gaining the smallest share of the vote since full records began: a mere 27 per cent.[17] The Conservatives were widely expected to enhance their majority in the parliamentary election from twelve to over one hundred.

Then something extraordinary happened.

Labour's draft manifesto was leaked, presumably with the intent of sabotaging the party's campaign. What the leak revealed was that, among other policies, it intended to bring privatised public services such as the railways, water, mail and energy back under public control, increase public spending, restore free education at universities, enhance the rights of workers and the unemployed, restrict the freedom of landlords to exploit their tenants and strengthen environmental rules and other public protections. This 'socialist programme', media pundits averred, signed the party's death warrant.

But it had the opposite effect. What the United Kingdom witnessed was perhaps the most dramatic political turnaround in modern democratic history. The policies in the Labour manifesto resonated widely. With the help of some of the Big Organising techniques I discuss in Chapter 9, Labour began to surge. Young people, many of whom had failed to participate in previous elections, began to flock to the party. When the country voted in June, Labour won 40 per cent of the votes and gained an extra thirty seats in parliament, while the Conservatives forfeited thirteen seats, losing their absolute majority, and spiralling into disarray.

With the manifesto, the Labour Party ceased to be a reactive, oppositional movement and became a propositional one. Jeremy Corbyn had been weak in opposition, but he was highly effective in proposition, connecting with voters in ways that the Conservatives found impossible to emulate. His policies represented a clean break from both the neoliberalism of his opponents and the triangulation of his Labour predecessors.

While these policies comprised a coherent programme, they did not, however, amount to a new political narrative. Labour offered a solid set of social democratic promises, which contrasted favourably with the neoliberalism that many people sought to reject. The next obvious step is to consolidate the party's renewed political identity by embedding these policies and others within a wider story of change. Then, I believe, Labour and parties like it, which seek to engage politically alienated people, could become irresistible.

4

Alienation

When politics, bereft of relevant stories, cannot connect with the lives of those it claims to represent, it contributes to the dominant condition of our age: alienation.

Alienation means many things. Among them are people's loss of control over the work they do; their loss of connection with community and society; their loss of trust in political institutions and in the future; their loss of a sense of meaning and of power over their own lives; and a convergence of these fissures into psychic rupture. In the political sphere, alienation leads to disengagement, and disengagement opens the way for demagogues.

In None We Trust

A marketing company called the Edelman Corporation compiles an annual 'Trust Barometer', based on surveys in twenty-eight countries. It has documented a collapse of the trust we invest in major institutions of all kinds since the financial crisis began. In two-thirds of the countries it studies, fewer than 50 per cent of respondents now trust mainstream business, government, media and non-governmental organisations to 'do what is right'.[1] Only 15 per cent believe that 'the present system is working'; 53 per cent do not.

The loss of trust cuts across social categories, affecting graduates and non-graduates; the prosperous and the poor; the well-informed and the poorly informed. Leadership in almost all fields is now an object of suspicion: people are much more likely to trust 'a person like yourself' than a chief executive or a government official.

Government is no longer seen as an effective force in delivering change; rather, it is widely regarded as 'incompetent, corrupt and divided': the least trusted of all institutions. The media comes next on this grim list: it is perceived as politicised and incapable of accuracy and impartiality. Globalisation and free trade agreements, the survey reveals, are broadly seen as hostile to human welfare. Trust, the Edelman Corporation observes, 'is now the deciding factor in whether a society can function'.

Detrimental Education

There are plenty of reasons for this collapse in trust. I believe that it begins for many people with an issue that seldom features in political analysis, but that is likely to play a major role in alienation: the nature of schooling.

I belong to the fortunate group whose form of intelligence – linear, analytical and hyperlexic – happens to be the kind that the education system rewards. I was told by the tests and the teachers that I was able. But as I became an adult, I began to notice something that was not evident at school: that my abilities were limited to a narrow range of tasks. Had I been tested in almost any area outside that narrow range, I would have failed, and perhaps I would have carried the expectation of failure throughout my life.

I also noticed that some of my friends could effortlessly perform cognitive tasks I found impossible. For example, one friend can precisely diagnose engine faults by listening – a skill that often astonishes professional mechanics. He has a spatial, navigational, system-based intelligence (as many people with dyslexia do). This variety of intelligence was neither tested nor rewarded at school. Despite his evident brilliance in certain fields, he was branded a failure.

I volunteer sometimes for an adventure learning charity that takes children from the poorest parts of London into stimulating environments. The first time I took a party of these children rockpooling, one boy stood out. He was observant, intuitive, full of ideas and curiosity, both physically and intellectually adventurous. He was often the first to put his hand up when I asked a question. While his answers were not always correct, they were always interesting, showing that he was thinking both creatively and logically. When I mentioned this to his teacher, her reply astonished me: 'I must tell him. It's not something he will have heard before.'

When a child like this is struggling at school, it is not the child who is failing, but the education system. I do not blame the teachers for this: they have to teach to the curriculum. The narrower the curriculum becomes – and the closer it is tailored to the expectations of commercial employment – the more children it will fail.

School, the first sustained contact with both the state and the professional classes, is, for many people, a humiliating and oppressive experience. They are made to feel inferior. They come to see the system as dismissive of their personalities and their intelligence. They find themselves at war with the representatives of this system: the teachers.

To add material injury to mortal insult, this miserable experience turns out for many people to be fruitless. As automation rips through the labour force, the safest jobs are now those that require creativity and social skills, as these are the hardest human attributes for machines to replicate. But education systems are still training humans to behave as if they were machines, setting them up for redundancy and failure.

Revolt Against Knowledge

This helps to inculcate a resentment towards the professional classes that finds political expression in polemics against the 'liberal elite'. This resentment is often reinforced by subsequent life experience. George Bernard Shaw famously remarked that 'all professions are conspiracies against the laity'.[2] Many people sense, often with justification, that their lives are being stitched up by managers, lawyers, journalists, bankers and a permanent governing class (installed in the offices of the IMF, the European Central Bank and national treasury departments) that cannot be dislodged by democratic means.

When I worked abroad – in Indonesia, West Papua, Brazil and East Africa – I met a number of European and North American development consultants, who sometimes had more letters after their names than in their names. They were paid vast per diems by the United Nations and the World Bank to fly into countries they had never visited before and produce plans for the 'development' of their peoples. I made a point of asking them about what they proposed to do, and why. Time and again, I discovered that they knew nothing about the lives of the people they had been sent to instruct: their arrogance was matched only by their ignorance. At those moments, I understood the anger that the 'liberal elite' attracts.

One of the many unfortunate consequences of this variety of alienation is a reaction against all experts, professionals and public servants, regardless of their value to society. Sometimes, especially on social media, the definition of the elite seems to expand to cover anyone with a degree, or even a salary.

Another consequence is that knowledge and expertise – the means by which suppressed people throughout history have emancipated themselves – become sources of embarrassment. For many years, the acquisition of knowledge was a route to individual and collective empowerment, and was strongly encouraged by trade unions and other organisations. Today, it is surrounded by suspicion. The era our intellectual forebears anticipated, in which the majority of humankind would be equipped with enough education and leisure to permit a general engagement with the great questions of life, has not materialised, and shows no sign of doing so. Instead, millions retreat into virtual worlds of fantasy and imaginary self-creation.

A prevalent anti-intellectualism is deliberately stoked by corporate lobby groups and their friends in the media, as anyone involved in the climate wars will testify. Algorithms are denounced, amusingly but dispiritingly, as Al-Gore-ithms. The use of models to forecast likely climate trends is ridiculed (though a substitute is never proposed – crystal balls, tea leaves, entrails?). The attack on scientific findings and those who produce them expands until it becomes an attack on learning itself.

The Coercive State

The suspicion attracted by expertise hardens as the role of government changes. During the Keynesian era, the state was the institution to which people turned for protection from exploitation and arbitrary power. Today it is perceived as an agent of exploitation and arbitrary power.

If you have work – especially if this work is insecure and contracted by the hour – you are likely to be subjected to a humiliating regime of impossible requirements, meaningless exhortations and panoptical monitoring. If you do not have a job, and try to obtain welfare payments, you are prey to a similar regime. Corporations and the state are experienced by many people as clubs raised on either side of them. If they turn in either direction, they will be hit. It takes an effort to remind ourselves that state power was once widely defended by working people as protective and enabling.

In his last book, *Ill Fares the Land*, the late historian Tony Judt observed that, as state services are both cut back and delivered by private companies, 'the thick mesh of social interactions and public goods' is reduced to a minimum, leaving 'nothing except authority and obedience binding the citizen to the state'.[3] So, paradoxically, if there is nothing that binds us together as a community or society, then we are utterly dependent upon the state. Governments that are too weak or discredited to act through their citizens are more likely to seek their ends by other means: by exhorting, cajoling, threatening and ultimately coercing people to obey them. The loss of social purpose articulated through public services actually increases the unrestrained powers of the over-mighty state.

Driven Apart

The activities that once brought us together now drive us apart. Where once we travelled to work on buses, trams and trains, now, partly as a result of massive state investment in roads coupled with the declining availability of public transport, many have little choice but to travel by car. It is not just that this means we stop talking to each other, but that when we drive, society becomes an obstacle. Pedestrians, bicycles, traffic calming, speed limits, the law: all become a nuisance to be wished away. The more we drive, the more bloody-minded and individualistic we become.

Traffic also damages social interaction at home. Studies in San Francisco and Bristol show a powerful inverse relationship between the number of vehicles using a street and the degree of social connectedness.[4] On streets with little traffic, the social engagement between neighbours is represented by a thick web of lines connecting the houses, often so dense that it resembles a woven cloth – this is the fabric of society. On streets with heavy traffic, the web is reduced to a few thin threads. The streets were once our commons, where children played and adults talked. But cars have occupied the space that people used for other purposes, drowned out conversation and – through noise, pollution and stress – driven us indoors. They slash through the social fabric of the street like a knife. The motorcar, I believe, though it is seldom recognised as such, is a potent agent of political change.

When we arrive at work, instead of the society of regular colleagues our parents knew, hot-desking, irregular shifts and zero-hours contracts ensure that, even if we are allowed to converse with our fellow workers, we might not know their names. People who would until recently have been enrolled in a company's workforce are now classified as independent contractors, doing the same jobs but without security, from one day to the next. The justifying rhetoric proposes that they have become entrepreneurs, free to enhance their livelihoods through enterprise. This is not quite how it works. In the United Kingdom, for example, self-employed contractors, on average, are now paid less than they were in 1995.[5]

The philosopher Byung-Chul Han argues:

Neoliberalism turns the oppressed worker into a free contractor, an entrepreneur of the self. Today, everyone is a self-exploiting worker in their own enterprise. Every individual is master and slave in one. This also means that class struggle has become an internal struggle with oneself. Today, anyone who fails to succeed blames themselves and feels ashamed. People see themselves, not society, as the problem.[6]

A war of all against all was not, as Thomas Hobbes proposed, our condition in the 'state of nature', but, driven by the intense competition encouraged by this fake self-employment, it is in danger of becoming our destiny. It develops into a war against ourselves.

The Mask the Machine Wears

Entertainment can also alienate us from each other. Where once we sat around the fire and talked and sang as we watched the flickering lights, today the lights and voices have been enclosed in a series of boxes. Television, while it tended to shut down conversation, at least was something that we watched, in the early days, together. Now we often watch it alone. We spend hours every day watching other people doing what we might otherwise be doing: dancing, singing, playing sport, even cooking.

What television tells us is that life is somewhere other than where we are. It encourages us to connect not with those around us, but with celebrities whom we will never meet, whose lives we are induced to believe we share.

The rise in celebrity culture is not an accidental or emergent feature of our age. It is the means by which distant and impersonal corporations connect with their customers and construct desire. It is hard for people to attach themselves to a homogenised franchise, owned by a hedge fund whose corporate identity consists of a filing cabinet in Panama City. So the machine needs a mask. It must wear the face of someone we see as often as we see our next-door neighbours. The role of people like Kim Kardashian is to exist in our minds, playing our virtual neighbour, to induce a click of recognition on behalf of the grey monoliths for which she works.

An obsession with celebrity displaces other concerns. A study in the journal *Cyberpsychology* reveals a sharp shift in the values expressed in popular culture across the course of just ten years (between 1997 and 2007).[7] In 1997, the dominant values (as judged by an adult audience) in the television shows most popular among nine-to-eleven-year-olds were community feeling, followed by benevolence. Fame came fifteenth out of the sixteen values tested. By 2007, when shows like *Hannah Montana* prevailed, fame came first, followed by achievement, image, popularity and financial success. Community feeling had fallen to eleventh, benevolence to twelfth.

A paper in the *International Journal of Cultural Studies* found that, among the people it surveyed, those who follow celebrity gossip most closely are three times less likely than people interested in other forms of news to be involved in local organisations, and half as likely to volunteer.[8] Virtual neighbours replace real ones. These people are also the least engaged in politics, the least likely to protest and the least likely to vote.

Now the boxes in which our entertainment is enclosed are in our pockets. Though the dreamworlds they contain are rich and fascinating, we tend to experience them alone.

Social media is double-edged: it is an excellent tool for creating connections, and a powerful weapon for breaking them. It intensifies social comparison to the point at which, having consumed all else, we start to prey upon ourselves. It allows us to quantify our social standing, and to see that other people have more friends and followers than we do. 'Beauty settings' on our phones retouch the photographs we post, sometimes automatically, making us look smoother and slimmer than we really are. We find ourselves competing not only with the idealised images of other people, but also with idealised images of ourselves.[9]

Research psychologists in the United States have discovered that, among pre-teens and young teenagers, the degree to which they used social networking sites predicted the degree to which their values were pro-social or anti-social: the more they engaged in social media, the less socially oriented their values became, shifting – again – away from helping other people and being connected to family life, and towards fame, image, money and status.[10]

When immersion in the virtual world is combined with a loss of contact with the physical world, reality slips and slides beneath us. We are permitted to believe simultaneously that anything is possible and that nothing is possible. People with few attachments to the tangible world are easily deceived.

The Age of Loneliness

When state provision, community, a sense of belonging and contact with physical reality are stripped away, all that is left is shopping.

The welfare state is widely blamed for promoting a culture of dependency and passivity. It would be foolish to deny that it can have this effect, though I would argue that this is greatly preferable to the extreme poverty, desperation and early death it has relieved. But it is curious that all the concern expressed by commentators about dependency culture is focused on this cause. Consumerism, television, cars, and the fetishisation of celebrities are also likely to reduce our mental or physical activity and undermine our self-reliance.

Consumerism stifles feeling, inducing a state of glazed compliance, dulling our concern both for the living planet it assaults and for other people. Like celebrity culture, it appears to render us politically inactive: lotus eating allows us to forget our losses. It ensures we become controllable and exploitable. It erodes common purpose: research published in the journal *Psychological Science* suggests that focusing on material goods and seeing ourselves as consumers rather than citizens strengthens our extrinsic values, intensifies our competitive urges and encourages us to behave selfishly.[11] Man was born free, and he is everywhere in chain stores.

As these trends in social breakdown reinforce each other, we are isolated from each other. We pay for this isolation with loneliness. The sustained emotional pain of separation can turn outwards: it is sometimes expressed as anger, misanthropy and further social withdrawal. Perhaps it is unsurprising that the word sullen derives from the old French *solain*: lonely.

When I make the mistake of reading the online comments below my articles – or anyone else's – the image that strikes me is of people trapped, alone in their cars, in a traffic jam, unable to see past the vehicle in front of them. Their anger and aggression is focused on the drivers ahead, and they lean on the horn, blaring pointlessly at them. Their isolation and frustration blind them to the context: the reasons for the jam, the reasons for their anger, the wider problems the snarl-up might reveal. Alienation, separation and stress suppress empathy, understanding, curiosity and cooperation. Deep thought becomes impossible. Rather than deliberating together to solve our common problems, we shout and shake our fists at each other.

All these trends reinforce the dominant story of our times: that we are governed by self-interest and driven by the desire to outcompete those around us. These might be inherent human tendencies, though the studies I referenced in Chapter 1 show that they are not our dominant characteristics. But we have arranged society in such a way that they come to the fore. We are assured that these antisocial traits are our greatest virtues, to be cherished, cultivated and defended against dastardly attempts to break down social barriers and work together. Atomisation and social collapse are celebrated as the preconditions for an entrepreneurial society.

The story of splendid isolation is so pervasive that when people suffer the psychological consequences of their disconnection from society, they might struggle to identify the cause. Plenty of exotic theories are proposed to account for the remarkable rate of mental health disorders now reported in many nations. But it seems to me that the erosion of community and our separation from others is sufficient to account for much of it.

We are alienated from each other, from the systems that govern our lives, from the spirit of inquiry, from the natural world, and from tangible reality. Socially, emotionally, intellectually and physically, we are in a poor state of health. The political consequences can be catastrophic.

The Crisis of Modernity

In his brilliant, incendiary book *Age of Anger*, Pankaj Mishra explains how people are radicalised by frustrated expectations.[12]

He argues that the extremism and terrorism emerging in many parts of the world are responses to a crisis of modernity that has been building for three centuries. The rise of commercial society, the global market economy, the nation-state and utilitarian rationality have been accompanied worldwide by violent social and political rupture.

We find this hard to see, he argues, because we subscribe to a sanitised history that records a steady progress across the industrial age of humane and tolerant values, placing the world wars 'in a separate, quarantined box' and treating Stalinism, fascism and Nazism as 'monstrous aberrations'. In reality, 'the history of modernisation is largely one of carnage and bedlam rather than of peaceful convergence'.

The first six decades after the Declaration of the Rights of Man was published by France's Constituent Assembly (in 1789) were defined in Europe by war, mob violence, repression and authoritarian rule. State and private terrorism, including the assassination of monarchs and prime ministers, continued through the nineteenth century. The rich world then exported this chaos, accompanied by resource grabbing and genocidal war, to the nations it colonised. The peace and stability rich nations have enjoyed since 1945 is anomalous and precarious.

Political and economic modernisation promised a utopia of equal rights and equal opportunities, a rationally ordered world in which old hierarchies and communities were overthrown, religion was replaced by reason, and history advanced purposefully, rather than meandering without pattern or direction. Through rational individualism and self-expansion, we would discover freedom and happiness.

The reality was not quite as promised: those who stepped,

full of expectation, into the new world, imagining that, having left their communities and shed their social identities, they would emerge in splendid isolation as the heroes of their own stories, found themselves confronted with gross inequalities of wealth, power and status, the crushing of political aspirations, police repression, torture and summary execution. In the gulf between the promise and the reality grew humiliation, and a sense of impotence, envy and rage: the afflictions of the 'superfluous men' portrayed in the novels of Pushkin, Dostoevsky and Turgenev. (An equivalent term today, coined by the blogger Anne Amnesia, is the 'Unnecessariat'.)[13] Their fantasies of violent revenge exploded into anarchist and nihilist terror. 'An anxious struggle for existence, a deep fear of "decadence" and emasculation, and messianic craving for a strenuous ethic, a New Man and New Order, went global in the late nineteenth century', Mishra writes. In the twentieth century this struggle consolidated into fascism and Nazism.

Mishra compares the alienated men of the nineteenth century with those being radicalised today, who gather around demagogues and extreme nationalist and religious movements. This radicalisation escalates in some cases into terrorism that strongly resembles nineteenth-century nihilist violence.

We tend to see far-right terrorists such as Timothy McVeigh, Anders Breivik and Thomas Mair (the murderer of the British MP Jo Cox) as the polar opposites of Islamic terror movements such as Isis. But, Mishra points out, they are united by a 'narrative of victimhood and heroic struggle between the faithful and the unfaithful, the authentic and inauthentic. Their blogs, YouTube videos and social media incarnations mirror each other, down to the conspiracy theories about 'transnational Jews', and identical strictures against feminism. 'There will be many more such men and women in the future, made and unmade by globalisation, unmoored to any specific cause or motive, but full of dreams of spectacular violence.'

As Hannah Arendt argued, it is in the powder of shattered communities that anti-politics swirls, raising dust devils of demagoguery and extremism.[14] When our broken social bonds are not replaced by new forms of connection, when a story of extreme individualism and self-interest mutes our generous, intrinsic values and emphasises instead a quest for power and status, we might find ourselves drawn to any mountebank telling tales of domination and victory.

Resurgent Fascism

Such crises do not solve themselves. I have lost count of the people who have assured me that demagogic governments will be so awful that people are bound to rise up, evict them from office in the next election, and replace them with the generous, inclusive politics we have all been waiting for. But this is not how it tends to work.

A useful way of understanding how people respond to political change is a concept coined by the biologist Daniel Pauly: 'Shifting Baseline Syndrome'.[15] It originally described our relationship to ecosystems, but it is just as relevant to politics. We perceive the situation that prevailed in our youth as normal and natural, and use it as the baseline against which we measure change. If ecosystems or political systems deteriorate, younger people, who know nothing else, regard that degraded state as normal and unexceptional – and so it continues. By this means, over the generations, we adjust to almost any degree of deprivation or oppression, imagining it to be natural and immutable.

When opposition parties are in disarray, when society is atomised and civic organisation is weak, when there is no compelling counter-narrative, demagoguery can continue unmolested. Its monstrosities are normalised, while those who seek to oppose it spiral into incoherence and despair, with isolated demonstrations that lead nowhere and grand statements disconnected from action. Donald Trump became president of the United States because his opponent provided no convincing or relevant alternative.

However extreme the policies of people like Trump become, there will be no effective response until those who oppose them adopt a new political story, and mobilise around it in a sustained and coherent fashion. If we fail to do so, the likely result is resurgent fascism.

5
Belonging

If alienation is the point on which our crises converge, belonging is the means by which we can address them.

The philosopher Kimberley Brownlee identifies three forms of belonging: belonging with, belonging to, and belonging in.[1] 'Belonging with' suggests an element of symmetry and reciprocity: we 'go together' with someone or something in the sense that 'Love and marriage . . . Go together like a horse and carriage'. 'Belonging to' could suggest that others may exercise power or ownership over us, but it also has positive connotations: a child who does not belong to a family is likely to experience this as a deep privation. 'Belonging in' suggests the ease we feel when we are at peace with our social setting or other elements of our surroundings. Together, these three forms of belonging help us to make sense of our lives and define our identities.

From infancy, we have a powerful need for all these modes of belonging: to be owned by a family and a society, to own a place within them that allows us to reciprocate, and to feel at ease with that place. It is this need for belonging that an effective politics recognises and recruits. Those who sought to change the world in the past were keenly aware of this.

Political Community

In Britain in the 1890s, alongside overtly political movements such as the Independent Labour Party, new thinkers launched ventures whose purpose was to create a community that worked both socially and politically.

For example, a magazine called *The Clarion* sought to 'make socialists' through the clubs it founded. As the historian David Prynn documents, it did so by stimulating what it called 'fellowship': group activities designed to create a sense of collective endeavour, while promoting the 'enlargement of the human personality' and the 'intellectual and moral regeneration of the working class'.[2] The clubs it founded also sought to provide relief from the drabness of working-class urban life, particularly by encouraging people to gather in the countryside.

Among these groups were cycling clubs, which organised mass bicycle rides called Clarion Meets. There were field clubs, which encouraged an interest in wildlife, folklore and architecture, in ways designed to 'counteract the cramming of the schools'. The Clarion Ramblers' Clubs and the Ramblers' Federation mobilised people to walk in the countryside, and to organise mass trespasses on land whose owners tried to shut people out. (These movements are celebrated in Ewan McColl's famous ballad, 'The Manchester Rambler'). In most cases – and through the Clarion Scouts and Clarion Vans – the organisers used the opportunity to distribute literature and advertise more overtly political movements and events.

The magazine also set up Cinderella Clubs, which provided food, clothing and entertainment to impoverished children. It offered free holidays and summer camps to the poorest of them. The Holiday Fellowship built on this work, emphasising the historical and literary interest of the places visited by its members, seeking to develop people's talents and to 'break down the barriers of race and class'. The Workers' Travel Association had similar aims.

These groups are considered by some historians to be as influential in the rise of British socialism as political parties were. As David Prynn notes,

> a change in social values was seen as a necessary pre-condition for a more general improvement in the condition of society. To make a healthier and more just society, it was first necessary to make people 'better', to alter human nature. In attempting to do this, it was believed that community living, fellowship and the expansion of the human personality would play a vital part.[3]

'Altering human nature' may sound frightening, in view of developments in the twentieth century. But all political movements, consciously or otherwise, attempt this. As Margaret Thatcher, who instinctively understood such matters, explained, 'Economics are the method; the object is to change the heart and soul.'[4] What she was talking about, though she did not express it in these terms, was shifting people along the value spectrum. The likely impact of her policies was to promote extrinsic values at the expense of intrinsic values. The likely impact of the fellowship societies established in the nineteenth and early twentieth centuries was to draw people in the other direction.

There were similar initiatives in 'Red Vienna' after the First World War, in Spain before and during the Civil War, in the United States in the first half of the twentieth century, and among contemporary or recent movements such as Occupy, the Movimento Sem Terra in Brazil, the Zapatistas in Mexico, Nuit Debord in France, the Indignados and Podemos in Spain, and the People's Science Movement in the Indian state of Kerala.

All these movements have emphasised, alongside the revival of community, intellectual development as a crucial component of politicisation. Those who organised the free evening lectures on relativity in Vienna and founded the Workers' Education Association in Britain understood the crucial role of the acquisition of knowledge. They believed – and to some extent demonstrated – that almost anyone could become intellectually active. Like cultural activities, popular education has been neglected by top-down social-democratic parties of late. This is another of the likely contributions to their loss of contact with those for whom they once spoke.

It is striking, reviewing this history, to see that even organisations now viewed as highly statist understood the importance of reviving community life. They knew that political life could not be built or sustained from the centre, and would not survive through politics alone. A population passively enjoying the fruits of other people's activism would eventually drift away. A political movement required a political community.

Taking Back Control

Before I continue, I want to make it clear that I do not seek to dismiss the importance of state provision. It has relieved levels of want and squalor that many people now find hard to imagine. But it can also, inadvertently, erode community, sorting people into silos to deliver isolated services, weakening their ties to society and their sense of belonging. Unless it is accompanied by a thriving community life, it can leave people dependent, isolated and highly vulnerable to cuts.

To create a social welfare system that has unintentionally (and perhaps inevitably) undermined self-reliance and mutual aid, then gradually to withdraw that system, depriving people of both sufficient state support and the community life it helped to supplant, feels like a cruel trick. We are left with the worst of both worlds: unmet material needs and a social void.

Top-down systems disconnected from community life can be blind to their wider impacts, however well-intentioned they may be: an example is brutal slum clearances that have pulverised communities. In isolation, they run the risk of creating a grey and dreary world. As the cultural theorist Jeremy Gilbert remarks, 'we might entertain time-travel fantasies of visiting Harlem in the 20s, Haight-Ashbury in 1967 . . . but who wishes they could spend a week in Surbiton, 1955?'[5] This was an era, in Britain, of universal provision, full employment and a strong belief in society and the state – in some respects a paradise from today's perspective. But, while some people do look back on it with fondness, others associate it with drabness and conformity.

It is clear to me that we need both: state provision and the revival of community. In fact, it is hard to see how we can sustain the former – or, for that matter, any redistributive or protective project – without the latter. Only through common purpose can we prevent the destruction of what we value, and promote the creation of what we want. This common purpose needs to be deeper and wider than the kind that political activism alone can deliver. As it happens, we are now blessed in many parts of the world with a resurgence of participatory culture that rivals the exuberance of the 1890s.

I would be sorry to give the impression that the only aim or purpose of this resurgence is to transform politics. I see it as a good thing in its own right, whether or not it leads to further outcomes. The revival of society remains an essential component of the benign transformation we seek, even if it could somehow be dissociated from economic and political revival. No further argument need be made for communities that are vibrant and attractive, that generate employment, that are environmentally responsible and socially cohesive, that generate a sense of all three kinds of belonging, and in which large numbers of people are involved in decision-making. Holiday and airline companies have worked hard to persuade us that living the dream means travelling the world, seeking novel experiences. But I suspect that what many people want above all else is a strong sense of home: to be embedded in a thriving and caring community.

But social revitalisation is also critical to the wider change we seek. If, as many political movements claim, people wish to take back control of their lives, this is a way to do it, without scapegoating immigrants, Muslims, Jews, foreign workforces, single mothers or the governments of other nations.

Participatory Culture

In cities and rural communities all over the world, we see an explosive revival of civic life, as people organise themselves to rebuild society from the bottom up. Among thousands of examples are community gardens, community shops, pubs and choirs, tea clubs, town festivals, development trusts, street parties and community lunches.

Time banking, which began in Japan, lets participants exchange the time they spend on social projects with other people.[6] They might, for example, earn some credits by helping an elderly neighbour with their shopping, then spend them by getting help with babysitting.

Food Assemblies allow people to order directly from local producers; the buyers then come together in one place to pick their orders up.[7] Transition Towns bring people together to reduce and transform their use of energy and revitalise local economies around green principles.[8] Men's Sheds, which originated in Australia, bring men together to make things in workshops.[9] In doing so, the men can begin to broach issues like loneliness and untreated health problems that they might otherwise have been reluctant to discuss.

Local currencies seek to anchor economies in the community, as the money cannot be spent elsewhere (their success so far has been mixed). New community groups founded by churches, mosques and other religious organisations have stepped into the social void, sometimes bringing people together across cultures and belief systems, sometimes setting them apart. Secular services, such as Sunday Assembly, replicate the work of religious services – allowing people to sing and talk together and build connections – without invoking a single belief system.[10] Community technology hubs help children and adults learn to code, explore technologies and invent new devices.

Groups like Playing Out, turning streets into temporary playgrounds, have begun to engage the whole community – including those without young children – as they inspire people to lobby for streets that are more hospitable to bicycles and pedestrians. Play sessions are used to collect toys and clothes for disadvantaged families.[11] Playing Out reports a potential shift in the children's worldview: seeing the adults taking action 'can influence their view of democracy and encourage them to feel they can change things and have a voice as they grow up'.[12]

Some places have gone further: a neighbourhood in Suwon, a city in South Korea, widened the pavements, created 'pocket parks', then banned cars for a month.[13] The local authority handed out bicycles and electric scooters (and taught people how to ride them). Cafés and restaurants spilled into the streets, and people began to connect in ways that were impossible before. Though cars were allowed back after the experiment, the community's attitude towards them had changed: the speed limit was cut by half, reducing the number of vehicles passing through, and street parking was restricted. The district now organises a car-free day every month.

Building Thick Networks

Turning such initiatives into a wider social revival means creating what practitioners call 'thick networks': projects that proliferate, spawning further ventures and ideas that were not envisaged when they started. They then begin to develop a dense participatory culture that becomes attractive and relevant to everyone, rather than mostly to socially active people with time on their hands.

A study commissioned by the London Borough of Lambeth sought to identify how these thick networks are most likely to emerge. A crucial aspect is that at least some of the projects must readily engage people who do not have much money, education or social confidence. Otherwise, participatory culture can become stuck in the 'exclusive, feel-good "facebook-urbanism" of the well-connected middle classes'.[14]

But a wide range of 'low-threshold, low-commitment' activities have the potential to draw almost anyone in. Ideally, they allow people to dip in and out without having to set aside much of their time and energy, or having to promise to participate for more than one session. Cooking and eating together is often a first step. It could be seen as fundamental to the establishment of society: the original meaning of the word companion is someone who breaks bread with another (*com* – with, *panis* – bread).[15] The exchange of cooking skills, a reduction in costs, and healthier eating are possible by-products of good fellowship.

Shared childcare, shared bulk buying, learning simple skills, sharing tools and equipment, and making and mending together are also useful early steps. Successful community projects are typically, like certain tech start-ups, lean and live: they start with very little money, and evolve rapidly through trial and error. They are developed not by community heroes working alone, but by collaborations between local people, ideally with a broad range of capacities.

Projects of this kind tend to spawn others, widening the opportunities to engage more people. When enough schemes have been launched, they catalyse a deeper involvement, generating community businesses, cooperatives and hybrid ventures, which start to employ people and generate income.

To reach the threshold at which participatory culture starts to ripple through the whole community, generating benefits even for those who are not directly engaged, the shift is likely to require help from the municipality. Such help, the Lambeth study argues, is highly cost-effective: supporting a thick participatory culture costs, in Britain, around £400,000 for 50,000 residents: roughly 0.1 per cent of local public spending. It is likely to pay for itself many times over, by reducing the need for mental health provision and social care, and by suppressing crime rates and recidivism, as well as alcohol and drug dependency. Mass participation 'would boost the protective factors' for people suffering from severe and multiple disadvantage 'far in excess of current levels'. The mutual aid such communities develop functions as a second social safety net.

A tipping point is reached when 10 to 15 per cent of local residents are engaging regularly.[16] Community then begins to solidify, causing a flowering of social enterprise and new activities. Participation comes to be seen as normal, and starts to draw in the rest of the population. As jobs are generated locally – for example, through community shops, bars, and energy-generating and distribution schemes – more people can work close to home, reinforcing a sense of attachment and ownership, and potentially making communities less transient. This process, the study reckons, takes about three years.

Mutual Reinforcement

Projects of this kind tend to make neighbourhoods more interesting, distinct and vibrant. They can embed people in the community who have previously been excluded or subject to prejudice. They can cure social isolation (those who join community organisations, according to one American study, are the social group among whom loneliness is least prevalent).[17]

They are likely to mobilise and reinforce our remarkable capacity for altruism and our deeply social nature. They could replace virtual, celebrity neighbours with real ones, weakening the felt need for celebrity culture. In some cases they might even draw people away from social media and into society – though I realise that for many this would stretch the bounds of the plausible. The effects on mental and physical health can be so profound that some doctors have begun 'social prescribing': referring people to community groups, rather than doling out drugs or recruiting specialist professional help.

Obviously, there are dangers here: community engagement can be used by governments as an excuse for social dumping. In Britain this has happened twice in recent years, through Margaret Thatcher's version of 'care in the community' and David Cameron's Big Society, both of which sought to use community as a substitute for the state, for functions it could not discharge. The protective mechanisms of state and society should be mutually reinforcing, rather than treated as alternatives.

While nowhere covered by the Lambeth study has yet reached the critical threshold, the most advanced case so far is Rotterdam. In response to the closure of local libraries, in 2011 a group of residents created a festival of plays, films, lectures and discussions in a disused Turkish bathhouse, which was renamed De Leeszaal ('The Reading Room').[18] Books, daily newspapers, computers, and tea and coffee were made available throughout the day. After the festival, the reading room became permanently embedded. It has become a meeting place where people can talk, read and learn new skills. With some help from the council, it soon began to spawn restaurants, workshops, care cooperatives, green projects, cultural hubs and craft collectives.

These projects inspired other people to start their own; one estimate suggests that there are 1,300 civic projects in the city.[19] New schemes are starting every week. Deep cooperation and community-building now feels entirely normal there, and has begun to address challenging and complex issues such as adult care, mental illness, debt and illiteracy. Empty shops have been filled; start-ups are proliferating. Microfunding and crowdsourcing groups have emerged to support them.

Rotterdam's participation culture has built trust between different communities, including between recent immigrants and longer-established residents. Volunteers for the Reading Room originate from seventeen countries, and range in age from ten to eighty-three. Both citizens and local government appear to have been transformed: the city council now collaborates with community groups to develop policies, and has asked them to train its civil servants.

There are other schemes with this potential. A project in the Spanish city of Zaragoza, called Estonoesunsolar ('this is not a vacant site') started with a plan to clean up vacant lots, following the real estate bust in 2008.[20] It soon began creating parks, playgrounds, bowling greens, basketball courts and allotments, generating 110 jobs in thirteen months.

Incredible Edible, which began as a guerrilla planting scheme in Todmorden, West Yorkshire, growing fruit and vegetables in public spaces and unused corners, has branched into so many projects that it is widely credited with turning the fortunes of the town around, generating start-ups, jobs and training programmes.[21]

Common Ground

To ask how participatory culture can revive political life is, in one respect, to miss the point: it is political life. It tends not to involve political parties or elections, though it plainly influences both. It creates social solidarity while proposing and implementing a vision of a better world. It generates hope where hope seemed absent. It reinvents local government through practice. It allows us to reach across political divides to establish common ground.

This, almost inexorably, can lead to a kinder public life. By reinforcing and spreading intrinsic values at the expense of extrinsic values, the revival of community is likely to generate a juster and more inclusive politics. It creates a sympathetic social environment in which the values and principles we articulate are more likely to be heard and understood. Could it also reanimate democracy?

The Home Crowd

In their fascinating but chilling book *Democracy for Realists*, the social science professors Christopher Achen and Larry Bartels argue that the 'folk theory of democracy' – the idea that citizens make coherent and intelligible policy decisions, on which governments then act – bears no relationship to how democracy really works, or could ever work.[22]

Voters, they contend, cannot live up to the folk theory's expectations. Most of us are too busy with jobs and families and troubles of our own. When we do have time off, not many of us choose to spend it sifting competing claims about recondite aspects of policy. Even when we do, we do not behave as the theory suggests.

Our folk theory of democracy is grounded in an Enlightenment notion of rational choice. This proposes that we make political decisions by seeking information, weighing the evidence, and using it to choose good policies, then attempt to elect a government that will champion those policies. In doing so, we compete with other rational voters, and seek to reach the unpersuaded through reasoned debate. In reality, the research they use suggests, most people possess almost no useful information about policies and their implications, have little desire to improve their state of knowledge, and have a deep aversion to political disagreement. We base our political decisions on who we are, rather than what we think.

In other words, we act politically not as individual, rational beings, but as members of social groups, expressing a social identity. We seek out the political parties that seem to correspond best to our culture, with little regard to whether their policies support our interests. Better information and civic education do not seem to help. The tiny number of people with a very high level of political information tend to use it not to challenge their own opinions, but to rationalise them. Political knowledge, Achen and Bartels argue, 'enhances bias'.

Perhaps we could see these tendencies as complementing our fondness for narratives: we interpret the world through our attachments, rather than through reasoned observation. We attach ourselves to stories and to social groups, and take the positions that seem to align with these attachments. In no aspect of our lives do we behave like the calculating machines – using cold reason to interpret and promote our self-interest – of economic mythology.

One conclusion we could draw from this work is that, if politics is an expression of social identity, we cannot change politics without changing social identities. I have argued that it is a change of social identity – through the dissolution of community and the atomisation and alienation that results – that has enabled the resurgence of extremism and demagoguery. By reviving society through stimulating a rich and thick participatory culture, we are likely to catalyse a transformation in outlook and attitudes.

As the psychology professor Dan Kahan argues, people tend to 'take their cue about what they should feel, and hence believe, from the cheers and boos of the home crowd'.[23] We create our political identities by looking around us and saying to ourselves, 'I am part of this and not part of that; these people are my allies and those people are my opponents.' If we perceive ourselves to belong to a community in which people work together to improve their lives and their neighbourhood, to enjoy each other's company and help each other, that perception is likely to shape our political self-image.

A political movement that articulates these values and connects directly with participatory cultures is likely to spread rapidly, as people take their political cues from those with whom they identify socially. In such a situation, a few effective organisers can shift the political choices of large numbers of people.

Public Luxury

A large-scale change in electoral choices is unlikely to occur passively: social organising needs to be accompanied by political organising. Chapters 8 and 9 explore how this might best happen. But places marked by lively participation are likely to develop certain characteristics in common, even without an active attempt to shape political choices.

Where a robust participatory culture develops, we might expect relations between recent immigrants and everyone else (in other words, less recent immigrants) to improve. Ecologists report that living systems that remain diverse and functional are better able to cope with disturbance than those that have lost many of their species and habitats. There is, perhaps, an analogy to be made here with human communities. The stronger they are, the better they can handle change.

Lively and confident communities with a wide range of economic and social opportunities are likely to harbour fewer prejudices against immigrants than do atomised collections of fearful, angry and alienated people. The process of participation tends to bring people into closer contact with those of other cultures, creating bonds of friendship and reducing the tendency to generalise and stereotype. If, as the Trust Barometer I mentioned in Chapter 4 suggests,[24] people are most likely to trust 'a person like yourself', then thicker community engagement, by creating a broader sense of who a person like yourself might be, could have the effect of expanding the scope of our trust.

As community education movements take off, knowledge can come to seem like something anyone can own once more, rather than an external imposition. Perhaps it will become easier for people to distinguish between expertise that is used to harm and expertise that is used to help.

Connected and engaged people are less likely to be trampled into the dirt than those who have become alienated and withdrawn. They are more likely to oppose changes that might damage their lives and their neighbourhoods, even if they are not working towards a clear political programme.

You can often spot places where community is thriving, even before you meet anyone, by their environmental quality. All over the world, weak communities with poor political representation are subject to the highest levels of pollution, noise and other forms of environmental stress. Disaggregated people are less able to resist plans to carve up their neighbourhoods with six-lane highways, to destroy public spaces, to segregate housing, to evict the poor in the name of regeneration. They are less able to fight for cleaner air, cleaner water, fair utility bills and good public transport.

Functioning communities are more likely to fight for public luxury – good parks, public buildings, sports facilities and other amenities – rather than allow the available space to be consumed by private and exclusive luxury. They are more likely to defend their streets as spaces that serve the community first and passing traffic second. They are more likely to resist the commercial forces that exclude children and the elderly from public places and public life. They might, as they have done in the past, even organise rent strikes when the costs of housing become too high.

The urban theorist Mike Davis points out that there is a 'consistent affinity between social and environmental justice, between the communal ethos and a greener urbanism':

> The cornerstone of the low-carbon city, far more than any particular green design or technology, is the priority given to public affluence over private wealth. As we all know, several additional Earths would be required to allow all of humanity to live in a suburban house with two cars and a lawn ... Public affluence – represented by great urban parks, free museums, libraries and infinite possibilities for human interaction – represents an alternative route to a rich standard of life based on Earth-friendly sociality.[25]

Digging In

Even before raising our political sights beyond the local community, it is possible to enhance this resilience. In the United States, a public interest law firm developed the concept of the 'community bill of rights'.[26] Some municipalities have the right to draw up their own set of local laws (the city Charter), which can be shaped by both elected officials and public petitions. Some communities, especially those threatened by fracking, have used the opportunity to establish bills of rights that put the protection of people and place above corporate profits. Companies that offend these rights can be fined. The protections these bills of rights offer can be overruled by recourse to state and federal law, but the unpopularity of attempts to do so has proved in some places to be an effective deterrent.

Inspired by this model, attempts to formalise the power of local organising have been made elsewhere, such as in the community charters developed in some parts of the United Kingdom. The process of developing such charters and bills of rights, like other aspects of participatory culture, can be a powerful means of bringing people together.

An effective method of producing these charters is through 'community conversations' of the kind developed by the group World Cafe.[27] The organisers create a hospitable setting that often looks like a traditional café with small round tables. Starting with the groups around each table, the theme is explored until the meeting agrees a common position. You could see such meetings as local constitutional conventions.

No More Losers

In his book *PostCapitalism*, Paul Mason points out that 'work – the defining activity of capitalism – is losing its centrality both to exploitation and resistance'.[28] In the absence of a stable, coherent labour force that can defend its interests and those of society as a whole, a new centre of both resistance and proposition is required. The most plausible candidate is local community, formed around participatory culture, building outwards to revive national and global politics.

This approach is neither quick nor easy (though it is a good deal quicker than wandering around in helpless circles, which appears to comprise the current strategy of most moderate political parties). But it has four obvious virtues.

The first is that no part of the process is wasted. Kindling participatory culture is beneficial whether or not it leads to political transformation. You could reach the end of a political life of this kind and tell yourself: 'We didn't take power. So all I've achieved is to bring people together, reduce loneliness, suspicion and fear, create jobs, entertainment and pleasant places to live, and increase the sum of human happiness. What a waste.'

The second virtue is that most of the steps towards change are pleasant. The same cannot be said of plans that mostly depend on political meetings.

The third is that the process of creating change is open to anyone, not just those who are employed in particular industries. That was a weakness of guild socialism and other labour-based political movements: they excluded people who did not belong to selected workforces, often shutting women, retired people, the self-employed and many others out of active politics. They sometimes created the impression that some people have a legitimate political role, while others are automatically disqualified.

The fourth is that you do not need to wait for anyone's permission to begin. While it is always a good idea to see what others are doing first, and join existing initiatives rather than replicating them, if you identify a gap that you can help to fill, you can start the process in your own street, tomorrow.

By making the community rather than the workplace the primary focus of our political lives, we might also address another potent issue: the rage and humiliation experienced by people who have been led to believe that their identity and validity arise from the jobs they do, only to discover that there are either no jobs at all, or only jobs that no self-respecting person would wish to take.

The problem with using work as a reference point for identity is that desirable identities become exclusive and hard to obtain. No such problem surrounds a sense of identity and validity arising from active citizenship. Anyone can join; anyone can make a contribution. Anyone can come to see themselves as a person who builds community, upon whom others rely for their well-being. There are no losers any more.

While people might take pride in a job that attracts high social status but causes tremendous harm to others, in this case, you can attach your pride and sense of purpose to something indisputably beneficial. Building community is a noble calling.

A Source of Strength

Reviving community is not a political panacea. By itself, it solves only some of our problems. Without other forms of political and economic engagement, of the kind I will discuss in subsequent chapters, it does not prevent the assets communities need to thrive – such as physical space and public budgets – from being captured for the exclusive use of a few. It does not cure the exploitations of the workplace or the attempts by some people to grab political power by undemocratic means.

Nor are local politics alone sufficient to change the world. Unless we are also engaged nationally and globally, our communities are at constant risk of destruction and dispersal. We can design, democratically and joyfully, beautiful streets and public spaces, while, unknown to us, governments collude with speculators to destroy everything we value: to them, we might be nothing but an obstacle to their grand designs. Unless we resist, they will sweep both us and our plans away to build their highways and office blocks and marinas and golf courses and gated compounds. Some governments, correctly perceiving cohesive communities as centres of resistance, will actively target them for destruction.

But, just as the workplace was once the solid ground from which national and international politics were launched, the revived community can become a source of strength on which we can build our wider movements. It is a lived example of the world we want to create, a repository of organisational techniques and experience, an inspiration to which we can keep referring while building our wider vision: a demonstration that another world is not just possible, but already exists.

6

Our Economy

I'm sorry, I must have misled you. Those aspects of life I described in the previous chapter – community action, community design, community ownership – appear to have been an illusion. None of them exist. No matter how hard I look, I cannot find them, at least in the standard economic models.

The following figure depicts a modern version of the famous circular flow diagram depicting the economy, whose first draft was produced by the author of the bestselling economics textbook of the twentieth century, Paul Samuelson.[1]

Several forms of human organisation are represented. But community is nowhere to be seen. When it is not in the picture, it is not in our minds. Missing from the diagrams, missing from the discussion, it is overlooked by most political and economic commentators.

Most political parties, of whatever persuasion, start from the same premise: that the fundamental political challenge is to find the right balance between the power of the market

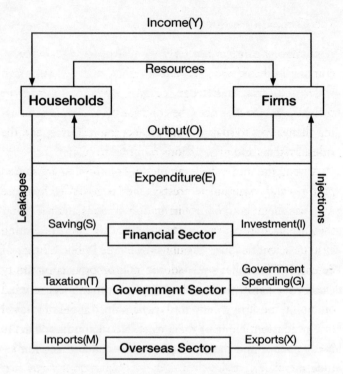

The circular flow diagram, after Samuelson

and the power of the state. Some parties insist that state powers be enhanced to protect people from the depredations of the market; others that the market should be released from the shackles of the state. Their shared premise is mistaken. The market alone cannot meet all our needs; nor can the state; nor can a combination of the two. Both, by rooting out attachment, have helped fuel the alienation, rage and anomie that breeds extremism. Over the past 200 years, one element has been conspicuously absent from both the economic models and most dominant ideologies, something that is neither market nor state: the commons.

The Common Treasury

A commons consists not only of a resource over which a community has shared and equal rights, such as land, fresh water, minerals, knowledge, culture, scientific research or software. It also describes the community of people organising themselves to manage and protect the resource, and the rules, systems and negotiations required to sustain it.[2]

Among the successful examples of commoning are shared pastures and community forests; fisheries governed by those who use them; community irrigation systems and the water they use; free software, such as the GNU or Linux operating system; scientific journals published by the Public Library of Science; Wikipedia; open-source microscopy; community energy cooperatives, which generate electricity from wind or sunlight; housing cooperatives; the Burning Man festival in Nevada; mutual insurance groups, like Broodfonds in the Netherlands; credit unions (financial cooperatives owned by their members); and crowdfunded and community-run taxi services, such as Ride Austin, in Texas, that replace commercial services like Uber.

While the commons is a complex concept, it has several consistent features. It is inalienable: in other words, it should not be sold or given away. Where it is based on a living resource, such as a forest or a coral reef, this obliges the commoners to consider its long-term protection, rather than the immediate gain that could be made from its destruction. The resource is not owned in the sense that private property is owned, yet the members of the community have property in it.

A commons makes sense of community. It provides resources that might help to secure the livelihoods of the

community's members, a focus for purposeful engagement, and the basis – as the resource belongs equally to
those who use it – for egalitarian relationships. It embeds
people in the lives of others: sustaining the resource means
cooperating with other people to develop rules, moral
codes and means of enforcing them. Thriving commons
are, I believe, crucial components of a politics of
belonging.

Daylight Robbery

If you mention this concept to policymakers, most of them
will either stare at you blankly or reject it with the phrase
used to condemn the sector for the past fifty years: the tragedy of the commons. This provided the title of a paper
published in *Science* magazine in 1968 by the biologist Garrett
Hardin.[3]

He argued that common property will always be destroyed,
because the gain that individuals make by over-exploiting it
will outweigh the loss they suffer as a result of its over-use.
He used the example of a herdsman keeping his cattle on a
common pasture. With every cow the man added to his
herds, he would gain more than he lost: he would be one cow
richer, while the community as a whole would bear the cost
of the extra cow. The paper had an enormous impact. For
governments and international agencies such as the World
Bank, it provided a rationale for the widespread privatisation of land.

But there was a flaw, which arose from the fact that Hardin
had no practical or even theoretical knowledge of how real
commons worked. He had assumed that individuals can

behave as selfishly as they like in a commons, because no one will stop them. In reality, traditional commons are closely regulated by the people who control them.

His thesis holds only where there is no community. The oceans, for example, managed by no one, are over-fished and polluted, as every user tries to extract as much from them as possible, and the costs of their exploitation are borne by the world as a whole. But the oceans are not a commons. They are a free-for-all.

His claims were thoroughly debunked by people with real knowledge of the systems he described, including the late political scientist Elinor Ostrom.[4] But facts are irrelevant when the theory is so useful. The myth of the tragedy of the commons has provided great service to both state power and private wealth accumulation, justifying the seizure of common wealth from those who once controlled it. Assets that were once held in common, or that could be held in common to the greater benefit of society, now supply companies and wealthy people with much of their capacity for profit-taking.

The process of enclosure – grabbing and monopolising other people's commons – began hundreds of years before Hardin's paper was published, as land was seized by kings and lords and colonists. When their commons were taken, communities were often scattered to the four winds. Enclosure continues today with the corporate patenting of assets previously owned by everyone and no one, such as our genetic material and chemicals derived from plants, and the private extraction of value from goods that were developed collectively: for example, technologies arising from government-funded research and the content published on online platforms, such as Google and Facebook, that is provided without charge by their users.

No sector is immune from the seizure and commercialisation of social wealth. To give one surprising example, among the most ruthless practitioners of monopoly capitalism are academic publishers.[5] Their content is provided by the academic commons: researchers freely collaborating to produce new work, generally financed by public money, which is then handed without payment to the publishers. The peer review process (the vetting of these papers by other researchers) and most of the editing are also provided without charge to the publishing companies. But the publishers then charge academic libraries vast fees for access, sometimes running to thousands of dollars per journal per year, and charge people who are unable to use these libraries $20, $30, even $50 to read one article. These practices have allowed the largest operators to sustain profit rates of some 40 per cent. Another term for enclosure of this kind is daylight robbery.

A primary purpose of most modern trade agreements is to secure and extend the intellectual property of transnational corporations, at the expense of those who must then pay for access. They are drafted, in other words, to prevent the sharing of resources. They permit corporations that have enclosed what might otherwise be common property to extract rent by creating artificial scarcity. The great commons of the Internet is now at risk of enclosure, as providers lobby to overthrow the rules ensuring net neutrality, whereby all traffic should be treated equally.[6]

The results of enclosure include the extreme concentration of wealth; the alienation of large numbers of people from the Earth's resources, the wealth we generate collectively, and the shared prosperity they could support; the erosion of community and the mutual aid that underpins it; and environmental destruction. Our relationships are reduced to the exchange of financial value, as both human life and the rest of the living world are commodified.

Extending the Commons

We do not need to call for the elimination of either state power or commercial markets to argue for the extension of the commons. A hybrid system, consisting of a market economy, state provision, the commons, alongside the fourth crucial sector of the economy, the household, would meet a wider range of needs and generate a stronger sense of belonging and meaning than the market, the state, or a combination of the two can deliver. Expanding the commons can act as a counterweight to the atomising, alienating forces now generating a thousand forms of toxic reaction.

Where a thriving commonweal stimulates a cooperative economy, the political effects can be profound. In his book *Viking Economics*, George Lakey portrays the widespread development of cooperatives in Sweden, Denmark and Norway as a response to the political extremism and economic dislocation of the 1920s and 1930s.[7] The farming, fishing, construction, retail and banking cooperatives people established helped to create social solidarity while the rest of Europe was falling apart, laying the foundations for the remarkable prosperity all three nations came to enjoy.

Enlarging the commons is likely to provoke conflict with both the state and corporations. Enclosed resources will not be surrendered easily or willingly; nor will corporate attempts to seize any new commons we might develop. For centuries, people have fought for the political space to develop their own forms of social and economic organisation. This struggle continues.

In some cases, extending the commons means reclaiming rights over assets that once belonged either to communities or to no one in particular. Some of these assets, such as land and the right to clean air, are essential to a widely shared prosperity. I will discuss this later in the chapter. In other cases, it is a matter of creating new commons and defending them from attempts at seizure.

This is what the government of Ecuador, responding to powerful social pressure, is seeking to develop through its Buen Vivir (good living) programme, at the core of which is a 'social knowledge economy'.[8] This is intended to create new sources of shared wealth, based on free and universal access to knowledge.

Such knowledge commons can be of great benefit to people who are deprived of access to learning by intellectual property rights and other proprietary barriers. But can they, as several optimistic accounts insist, be directly translated into income and livelihoods? Some authors claim that the free content being exploited commercially by platforms such as Facebook and Google could be monetised with the help of verification technologies (such as the blockchain ledger), and the profits currently monopolised by these behemoths distributed to the people who provide the content.

This seems unlikely to me. The tendency in many cases is surely towards free use and free access, rather than towards the distribution of commercial benefits. More plausible, for me, is Paul Mason's account of the development of an information economy steadily eroding commercial value as it replaces the artificial scarcity of information goods with natural abundance.[9] Free information produced by collaborative production, he argues, will drive out commercial commodities.

This presents as many problems for those who see peer-to-peer production as the means of creating a new commercial sphere as it does to the current generation of knowledge monopolists, using brute power to sustain their intellectual property rights. The commons might enhance our well-being, as we use their value directly, but only some aspects of this well-being translate into money.

Who Owns What?

So how, in an ideal world, would we best determine how the use and value of resources should be distributed between state, market and commons? I would formulate the basic principles guiding such decisions as follows. Those forms of value that are generated through work, enterprise and ingenuity properly belong to the people who produce them. In many cases, this means that value accrues to individual citizens and private commercial enterprises. (The state, to discharge its duties, is entitled to tax part of this gain.) Those resources that are not created by people, or that are created by society as a whole, should most appropriately be managed as commons, and the value arising from them shared by a community.

The role of the state is then to manage resources that are either too large or too diffuse to be responsibly stewarded by private concerns or commoners; to provide services and infrastructure that cannot be as fairly or comprehensively delivered by either the market or the commons; to set and enforce common standards for environmental and social protection; and to address deprivation by transferring wealth from richer to poorer communities through tax and public investment. The state ensures that all economic sectors – market, commons, household and public sphere – can prosper without unduly intruding upon each other.

This is easily stated, less easily implemented. Value does not always divide neatly between 'natural' and 'acquired' property, to use Thomas Paine's distinction,[10] or between earned and unearned income. For example, it is not always easy to discern how much of the price of a plot of land arises from the underlying value that the owners did not create, and how much is generated by the works (such as the construction of a house) they commissioned – though in most cases we can make a reasonable guess, based on average prices across the district.

Nor is it always easy to determine which community should fairly benefit from a natural or common resource, who qualifies as a member of this commons, and how they should best be compensated for the use of their resource. Producing a system that conformed neatly to the principles I have just proposed would require the untangling of centuries of ownership, probably catalysing major conflict.

Whatever we do to create a fairer, more inclusive system will be messy, incomplete and subject to constant negotiation. I see this as a good thing. The absolute application of principles is a formula for either failure or tyranny. But we can go some of the way.

From the Ground Up

Let us begin with a resource on which plenty of we
based, both literally and metaphorically: the land. Land
asset that no one created, but it has been acquired in large
part by a minority, who can thus charge others for its use. We
are punished in perpetuity for surrendering it, through the
extraction of rent (unearned income) by those who have
enclosed it. We enhance the proprietors' unearned income
by providing, through our taxes, the infrastructure and
services that raise the value of their land.

This is how a dangerous subversive explained the problem, in 1909:

> Roads are made, streets are made, services are improved, electric
> light turns night into day, water is brought from reservoirs a hundred
> miles off in the mountains – and all the while the landlord sits still.
> Every one of those improvements is effected by the labour and cost
> of other people and the taxpayers. To not one of those improvements
> does the land monopolist, as a land monopolist, contribute, and yet
> by every one of them the value of his land is enhanced. He renders
> no service to the community, he contributes nothing to the general
> welfare, he contributes nothing to the process from which his own
> enrichment is derived . . . The unearned increment on the land is
> reaped by the land monopolist in exact proportion, not to the service,
> but to the disservice done.

Who was this anarchist? Winston Churchill.[11] He was one in
a long line of eminent thinkers to have recognised this problem, a problem that today most politicians affect to ignore.
Those who buy land compensate only the previous owner,

rather than the other people deprived of its value. The property taxes landowners pay tend to represent a small fraction of the value they extract from the rest of us. On the whole, unearned wealth is taxed in much lower proportion than earned income – a perversity that reflects the power of those who harvest it.

The fees the owners of land extract greatly raise the cost of living for the rest of society – in ways that are obvious, such as the payment of extortionate rents for housing, and in ways that are less so, such as the incorporation of the inflated cost of business rents into the price of the goods those businesses sell. Governments often rent property from the private sector, and the high levies they pay raise the cost of public services. The absence of fair property taxes means that more money must be extracted by other means, shifting taxation from propertied people to the unpropertied, and from unproductive sectors to productive activities.

Part of the money we pay to use property fairly compensates owners for the improvements they have made, such as the buildings they construct and renovate. But much of it – the great majority in some locations – pays for the speculative value. We pay twice: to build the infrastructure and public assets that raise the value of the land, and to compensate the owner for the value we have thus created. Were we not immersed in this system, and therefore unable to see it, we would immediately apprehend it as an outrage.

In his book *Land*, the community organiser Martin Adams proposes that those who use the land exclusively should pay a 'community land contribution' as compensation.[12] The principle is long-established. Adam Smith pointed out that 'ground-rents are a still more proper subject of taxation than the rent of houses. A tax upon ground-rents would not raise the rents of houses. It would fall altogether upon the owner of the ground-rent, who acts always as a monopolist, and exacts the greatest rent which can be got for the use of his ground.'[13] But community land contribution is a more accurate term than either ground-rent taxation or land-value taxation, as this is not a tax, but a fee for services rendered: a return to the public of the benefits we have donated to the landlords.

This could be used as the first stage in a transition towards community ownership. Community land contributions create a fund that can be administered by either local government or a community land trust. When land is sold, either the trust or the local authority can use the fund to buy it and then charge people or companies for its exclusive use. Alternatively, the fund could be used to provide finance for those who wish to buy homes and businesses, in return for which the owners pay a monthly or annual sum for the use of the land on which they are sited. In either case, the value of the land is returned to the community.

Such measures are likely to make the ownership of buildings more accessible, as the value of bricks and mortar is separated from the value of the land: no longer will people be saddled with unpayable mortgages and ridiculous rents. They prevent speculative land hoarding: to pay their community land contribution, which will be highest in prosperous cities, landowners would need to bring their property into active and efficient use, so that it generated revenue. The land contribution ensures that the most valuable real estate – in city centres – is developed first, discouraging urban sprawl and increasing urban density, which makes cities more functional and less environmentally damaging, and ensures that services are easier and cheaper to deliver.

These policies would bring down land prices and prevent speculative property bubbles of the kind that regularly destroy economies and livelihoods. They would reduce the price of goods and services. Unlike many forms of tax, which appear to be discretionary for the very rich, a community land contribution is unavoidable: you cannot shift your land to Panama or the Cayman Islands. These measures help us to see the land as a common resource that belongs to us, and to which we belong.

From the Sky Down

Similar principles could be applied to many common assets that private businesses and individual users currently take either freely or for very low fees, such as the atmosphere, minerals, wild fish, forests, water and the electromagnetic spectrum. Drawing on the work of the legal scholar Carole Rose,[14] the economist Peter Barnes has proposed a series of common wealth trusts to own and manage common property, ranging from watersheds and transport systems to the global atmosphere.[15]

These bodies would hold resources in trust for future generations, set the level at which they can be used (ratcheting it down where they are already overexploited), and then auction the limited rights of use they have established. The tighter the environmental constraints, the further the price of usage is likely to rise, encouraging the development of less resource-hungry technologies and business models.

Perhaps the most ambitious proposal of this kind is for a common sky trust. This would be a global body, owned by the world's people, that would hold the atmosphere in trust for future generations, and rapidly reduce the number of permits to pollute it with greenhouse gas emissions. These could be auctioned to polluting industries positioned as far upstream as possible, to minimise the number of transactions, such as oil refineries, coal washeries, gas pipelines and cement and fertiliser works.[16] As the price rose, it would create a powerful incentive to abandon fossil fuel consumption in favour of low-carbon energy.

So how should the money such commons generate best be used? The authors Angela Cummine and Stewart Lansley have, independently, suggested the creation of social wealth funds.[17] These would be similar to the sovereign wealth funds some nations have amassed. Sovereign wealth funds are often used only as investment arms. Social wealth funds, by contrast, have the explicit purpose of distributing wealth (the closest existing models are the sovereign funds run by Alaska and Norway, which disburse oil revenues).

Such funds could operate at different levels. Local commons trusts could use their income, as they do today, either to distribute money directly to their members or to create community assets (such as youth clubs, libraries, parks and playing fields). Global trusts (such as a sky trust) could use the money they generate for environmental restoration and the development of greener technologies, or could distribute it among the world's people as a global dividend, as the philosopher Thomas Pogge suggests.[18] And national funds – well, this is where the idea could mesh with the next component of an inclusive economy.

The Distributive Economy

Though it has been discussed for centuries, a universal basic income (UBI) was treated until recently as a marginal and outlandish idea. UBI is an income paid to every adult – and, in some proposals, every child. It is unconditional: in other words, unlike some forms of social security, it does not depend on qualifications such as poverty or attempts to find work.

The idea is now moving into the mainstream partly because both employment and unemployment benefits are widely perceived to be failing. The insecurity and poverty experienced even by those who can find work, combined with a coercive and often draconian welfare state, has driven thinkers and politicians to explore alternatives.

Parts of Finland, the Netherlands, Namibia, Spain, France, Canada and Scotland have run small-scale, experimental projects: this is always, in my view, the right way to begin. An experiment in Kenya channels foreign aid directly into the pockets – or, more precisely, the phones – of the poor.[19] Already, most of the world's people, including many of the poor, have mobile phones, which could enable them to use mobile banking services. Foreign aid is currently under attack in many rich nations, as its opponents argue that much of it disappears into the offshore bank accounts of corrupt officials, or is swallowed by administrative costs and white-elephant schemes. While these charges are often exaggerated, they tend to contain some truth. In many cases, aid might be both more effectively deployed and more politically sustainable if it went directly to the intended beneficiaries, in the form of a basic income. (The danger here, though, is that it may leave essential state services, such as health and education, underfunded.)

In a trial of UBI in the Indian state of Madhya Pradesh – whose levels of poverty ensure that even small payments can make a big difference – strong improvements were seen after six months in health, nutrition and school attendance.[20] Replacing India's perverse public subsidies and complex, corrupted welfare programmes with a universal basic income should result in a significant increase in well-being. But the effects are likely to become weaker in nations whose people are richer, and whose administrative systems are more effective.

A UBI does not cure all ills (and it could create a few). Some of the claims made for the proposal are inflated: it is unlikely to provide a full substitute for social security payments or housing benefits in the rich nations, or for employment in any nation. But it does have the potential to relieve extreme insecurity; to grant people some breathing space between jobs, or while they try to develop new careers or start their own businesses; to de-fang intrusive and punitive regimes of benefit sanctions; to reduce fraud; to raise people's confidence as they negotiate with their employers; and to spring people out of the poverty trap (in many nations, because social security payments decline rapidly as people take on even low levels of work, returning to employment scarcely pays). The absence of means testing and other assessments could make it cheaper to administer than other forms of welfare.

But there are significant hazards. One possibility is that employers would seek to use this income supplement as an opportunity to hold down wages and expose their workers to greater insecurity – in effect, passing part of their employment bill to the state. Another danger is that UBI might become a means by which more progressive forms of wealth distribution – public money received disproportionately by the poor – are dismantled. This is the basis of its appeal to some neoliberal thinkers, who enthuse about its potential to destroy targeted state provision.[21] The basic income, they argue, could be used as a kind of voucher scheme to purchase services from private companies, making the welfare state redundant. Unless very large amounts of money were spent on UBI, or we were to accept a major decline in the quality of public services, it is hard to see how it could fulfil this role. Even if they do not buy the whole programme, some governments are likely to treat UBI as a substitute for, rather than a supplement to, the social security system.

The basic income could be financed through an expansion of income tax or other existing sources of revenue. But the idea of building a national social wealth fund from the fees charged to those who use assets they did not create is appealing for several reasons. It is likely to be more politically acceptable than an extension of existing taxes. It prevents the increment in people's incomes from being captured by rent-seekers. And there is a pleasing symmetry to this approach, which helps people to appreciate both elements of the programme: universal assets are used to fund universal benefits. There is a sense, at both ends of the system, that it belongs to us.

But there is a hazard here as well. Several of the proposals I have read, including the original version (Thomas Paine's, in his 1797 essay *Agrarian Justice*),[22] suggest pooling the money provided by community land contributions into a single national fund to supply the UBI. They do not seem to have noticed that they propose to replace one form of enclosure with another. Under this plan, assets that could be deemed to belong to local communities are de-privatised only to be nationalised. This programme eliminates the local interest, and the motivation of local people to protect and nurture their common property. The commons – often the most democratic, just and responsible means of owning and managing such assets – is here replaced by the state.

Drawing on the work of many others, I propose the following model. The state taxes the communities that benefit from very high land values (in the metropolitan centre, for example), but not the communities whose assets produce little income. This reflects its legitimate role in redistributing wealth from richer to poorer communities. The tax it exacts contributes to the national social wealth fund. So does the income from common assets that are best administered nationally, such as licences to use parts of the electromagnetic spectrum.

The fund could be supplemented with a tax on financial transactions (of the kind proposed by James Tobin),[23] and taxes on other sources of unearned wealth, which could – as Yanis Varoufakis, the economist and former Greek finance minister, proposes – include shareholdings.[24] The social wealth fund, by pooling these assets both spatially and temporally (smoothing fluctuations in income from one year to the next), would provide a steady, inflation-proofed basic income to every resident of the nation.

The Vista

The measures discussed in this chapter might enhance the distribution of wealth and our sense of belonging. But, on their own, they do not guarantee either general prosperity or the protection of the world's ecosystems and natural processes, on which we and all other life-forms depend. It is possible to envisage a fully participatory, socially just economic system that still destroys the world's ecosystems. To defend the long-term interests of humanity and all other living beings, we must take a wider view.

7

Framing the Economy

For mainstream economists, the living planet is an afterthought – or, worse, a prayer. The prayer goes something like this:

> Dear God/Invisible Hand/Spirit of Friedrich Hayek,
>
> May our quest for endless economic growth somehow coexist with a viable future for the world's living systems and the people who depend on them. We have no idea how this might happen, but the economy works in mysterious ways.
>
> Amen.
>
> PS: Don't worry if you've got too much on; it's not such a big deal.

Our impacts on the biosphere – the frail membrane in which life occurs, which envelops the dead rock of planet Earth – are treated as externalities. The living world exists outside the realm of market exchange, and therefore outside the models. Or it is reduced to just another component of the

economy. As the neoliberal economist Milton
put it, 'Ecological values can find their natural
the market, like any other consumer demand.'[1] The
ward fact that all human life would immediately end
without it is someone else's problem.

To mainstream commerce, the Earth is both loot and
dump. Commercial activity, broadly speaking, consists of
extracting resources from a hole in the ground on one side of
the planet, inducing people to buy them, then dumping them
a few days later in a hole in the ground on the other side.
Whether or not they were useful to those who purchased
them is irrelevant: if marketing can persuade people to part
with their money in exchange for goods, the interests of
humanity have been served. The faster we do this, the more
successful economic life is deemed to be, and the greater is
the sum of human progress.

To mainstream politicians, the living world (denoted by an
alienating term that conveniently creates no pictures in the
mind: 'the environment') is something their advisers tell them
they should appear concerned about. Whatever that environment thing may be, and they never seem too sure, they must
look grave and shake their heads and explain that the crucial
task is to ensure that we act sustainably. They have little idea
of what this means, either. You can tell by the way the language
shifts. First they talked about 'sustainability'. Then it became
'sustainable development'. Then it evolved into 'sustainable
growth'. Then it became 'sustained growth'. Sustainability
and sustained growth are antithetical concepts. But no one
seems to have noticed: they are used interchangeably.

To the mainstream media, the environment is what blow-
hards talk about. Lip service must still be paid, but only

when there's a meeting about it featuring Very Important People. What then counts is what these people say to each other, and who stands where in the photo, and what this meeting might mean for the next meeting. Occasionally a journalist reports from somewhere that is not a hotel or conference centre, such as a rainforest or glacier or coral reef – somewhere no one in their right mind would wish to visit unless it involved a luxury safari lodge, ideally with spa and sauna. They will say the usual thing about everything turning to dust. It will be dumped at the end of the news programme, between a crucial report on the brand of shoes the prime minister favours and the football results. It will be picked up by no other journalists, as they will be too busy poring over what one very important person said to another in an overheard conversation in a restaurant, and what this might mean for the career of a third, and whether it might affect the results of the election in three years' time.

To most people, who are not economists or politicians or journalists, the state of the living planet features as a real but remote concern, dimly perceived through the gauze of daily life. Something to worry about, certainly, once the mortgage has been paid and the kids have left school and we have worked out what the hell to do about our pensions. Probably the best time would be never. But right now it is all too complicated, and it can't be that much of an issue anyway, if no one's stopping us from buying that bigger car we fancy, or eating the fish those people say are almost extinct, or washing our hair with stuff made from palm oil. If it were that big a deal, 'they' would do something, wouldn't they? Occasionally, when disaster strikes, the dull apprehension surges into perplexity and alarm, but this abates as fast as the floodwaters recede. Some people switch from denial (it's all nonsense, nothing's going to happen) to resignation (it's too late to do anything, we're doomed) without pausing for a moment's resolve (it's real, and we must act).

To be an environmentalist, to see what others refuse to see, is to struggle every day against hostility, denial and, above all, indifference. It is to find yourself fighting almost everyone in a position of power. It is to find yourself locked in a constant cycle of determination and despair.

I could recite the long and familiar list of horrors: the natural marvels eliminated for a mess of pottage; the shocking, disorienting speed with which living systems are being snuffed out. But this approach, as I know from bitter experience, tends not to engage people but to repel them. Instead, I will mention just one issue that exemplifies our relationship with the natural world.

Disposable Planet

The state of our soils features in the media and political life even less often than other environmental issues. When it does, it is usually expressed in financial terms. In England and Wales, for example, according to a parliamentary report, the loss of soil 'costs around £1bn per year'.[2] When we read such statements, we absorb the implicit suggestion that this loss could be redeemed by money. After all, monetary figures are meaningless unless the goods they measure can be so redeemed. The presumed financial loss (whose quantification is as dodgy as most such attempts to price the biosphere) distracts us from the real issue: that this is the basis of our subsistence. When the soil goes, we go with it. The aggregate of £1 billion of soil lost this year, £1 billion lost next year, and so on, is not a certain number of billions. It is the end of civilisation.

The UN Food and Agriculture Organisation uses a more relevant metric. At current rates of soil degradation, it reports, the world on average has sixty more years of harvests.[3] A combination of powerful machinery and the drive for immediate profit rather than long-term protection incites farmers to compact and churn the soil and leave it exposed at crucial moments, whereupon rain or wind strips it from the land. To keep up with global food demand, the UN estimates, 6 million hectares (14.8 million acres) of new farmland will be needed every year. Instead, 12 million hectares a year are lost through soil degradation.[4] In an era in which everything is treated as disposable, we use it, lose it, and move on, trashing rainforests, wetlands, savannahs and other precious habitats to mine what lies beneath.

This is not an unanticipated side effect of the system; it is the system. In *The Constitution of Liberty*, Friedrich Hayek argues that

> 'soil mining' may in certain circumstances be as much in the long-range interest of the community as the using up of any stock resource . . . Such resources share with most of the capital of society the property of being exhaustible, and if we want to maintain or increase our income, we must be able to replace each resource that is being used up with a new one that will make at least an equal contribution to future income. This does not mean, however, that it should be preserved in kind or replaced by another of the same kind, or even that the total stock of natural resources should be kept intact.[5]

In other words, as Hayek explains, 'There is nothing in the preservation of natural resources as such which makes it a more desirable object of investment than man-made equipment or human capacities.' Soil should be treated like any other form of capital: disposable and exchangeable for money. Our sole duty to each other is to maximise income. As long as we replace the soil we mine for profit with something else – a new factory for example – its exhaustion is of no account. What happens when we exhaust the soil everywhere appears, strangely, to be beyond the scope of his analysis.

Let's Move to Mars

But plenty of people propose an answer. Seldom does a week go by without someone writing to me to explain that when we have squandered this planet's capacity to support us, we can abandon it and move to another one. Earth itself should be treated like a plastic cup or a paper towel: to be thrown away when it is of no further use. (Or, to be more precise, we should throw ourselves away – into space. Perhaps it would be more accurate to say that we see ourselves as disposable.) This belief is the ultimate negation of belonging.

People who would consider the idea of living in the Gobi Desert intolerable – where, a realtor (estate agent) might point out, there is oxygen, radiation-screening, atmospheric pressure and one g of gravity – rhapsodise about living on Mars. People who blithely envisage the collapse of our biosphere imagine that we will escape the power, greed and oppression that could cause it by relocating into orbiting pressure vessels controlled by technicians, in which we would be trapped like tadpoles in a jam jar. The enthusiasm for planetary abandonment is not restricted to a far-out fringe: NASA has published papers presenting it as a thrilling prospect.[6] This is how far the detachment from physical reality has advanced. This what is delivered by a system that insists we are subject to no resource constraints.

Invisible Hands

Under the current economic programme, success is measured by the expansion of commerce, regardless of the net effects on our well-being. Expansion can proceed only by finding new ways of persuading people whose needs have already been met to part with their money. It is inevitable therefore that the products on sale become more preposterous with time.

You can now buy wigs for babies, to allow 'baby girls with little or no hair at all the opportunity to have a beautifully realistic hair style';[7] an egg tray for your fridge that syncs with your phone to let you know how many eggs are left;[8] a gadget for scrambling them – inside the shell;[9] a snow sauna, in which you can create a winter wonderland with the flick of a switch;[10] a refrigerated watermelon case on wheels, indispensable for picnics;[11] pre-peeled bananas, in polystyrene trays covered in cling film (just peel back the packaging); a smart phone for dogs, with which they can take pictures of themselves.[12]

For this ingenious rubbish – much of which is unlikely ever to be used, since its primary purpose is to trigger an impulsive reflex among bored consumers – we have exchanged a world of natural wonders: coral reefs and ice sheets, rainforests and wetlands, whales and rhinos, bees and birdsong, streams and meadows, and all the tiny marvels whose loss is seldom recorded. For this junk, we have reduced our chances of survival. Economic growth – the primary measure of success, whose absence, even in the richest nations, is deemed a social and political crisis – depends on the expansion of demand for pointless goods and services. The accelerating use of materials – which requires the accelerating degradation of ecosystems – is recorded as a triumph; the reduction of resource use as failure. To succeed, we must destroy ourselves.

It is clear that we cannot protect the living planet, our sense of place and belonging on it, and our own well-being, unless we change the frame through which we see it, and through which we see ourselves. A frame is the mental structure that shapes the way in which we apprehend an issue. It is hard to solve a problem from within the frame that created it.

The genius of Kate Raworth's book, *Doughnut Economics: Seven Ways to Think Like a 21st-Century Economist*, lies in her comprehensive reframing of the subject.[13] As she reminds us, drawing on the work of the cognitive linguist George Lakoff,[14] refuting a dominant frame serves only to reinforce it. To displace it, we must create a new one. She does this in the most direct fashion: by redrawing the graphs through which economics sees the world. Her purpose is to 'make assumptions explicit and blind spots visible'.

She points out that the circular flow diagram – a version of which I reproduced in the last chapter – portrays the economy as a flow of income on an otherwise blank page. Energy, society and power relations: none of them appear in the picture. It creates the impression that the economy is a closed, self-generating loop.

In reality, matter and energy flow into the economy and out again. The fundamental resource flow is not the money circulating within it, but the energy moving through it. Here is Raworth's depiction.

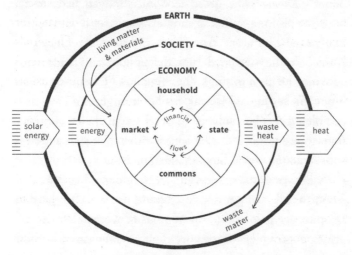

The embedded economy

Her diagram obliges us to recognise that all economic activity is embedded both within the Earth's living systems and within society. It belongs to us and belongs to the world in which we live. It also reminds us that we are not just workers, consumers and owners of capital. We are also citizens, members of families and communities, volunteers and cooperators. And we emerge from a sphere that, like the commons, economics has characteristically neglected: the household.

Unless children are loved, looked after, fed, taught basic skills at home and taken to school, they will have no means of joining the workforce, except at the lowest level, when they grow up. Unless workers are healthy and emotionally stable and have some order in their lives, they might not be able to remain in employment. The household, identified by some thinkers as the core economy, makes everything else possible.

As Katrine Marçal reveals in her book *Who Cooked Adam Smith's Dinner?*, the great economist moved back to the house of his long-suffering mother, Margaret Douglas, who had raised him alone from birth, to write *The Wealth of Nations*.[15] She sustained him throughout this endeavour, cooking and cleaning and relieving him of other tasks. Were it not for her unpaid labour, his book might not have been completed. Yet he managed to overlook such vital contributions to economic life. The hands with which she swept and cooked and made his bed remained invisible.

By ignoring this sphere, and treating unpaid labour as no labour at all, economists downgrade the work of women. Despite the gains made by feminism, women remain the principal providers of the core economy: the carers without whom everything falls apart.

Circle of Life

Raworth, whose work is the most considered and far-reaching of the materials I have read while researching this book, explains that, during the twentieth century, economics stopped articulating its goals. As a result, it was overtaken by an implicit objective: growth.

Growth in GDP is treated as the answer to everything, even before the question has been asked. It is supposed to cure poverty, debt, trade imbalances, inequality, political conflict, even environmental degradation. But as the man who standardised the measurement of growth, Simon

Kuznets, explained, 'The welfare of a nation can scarcely be inferred from a measure of national income.'[16] He pointed out that it ignores the value of the core economy and measures only annual flow, rather than stocks of wealth.

Raworth proposes that we rethink economics from first principles, beginning by articulating our objectives, then determining how the economy can best serve them. Her chosen goal is simply stated: 'meeting the needs of all within the means of the planet'. And from this objective, she produces her next, and crucial diagram.

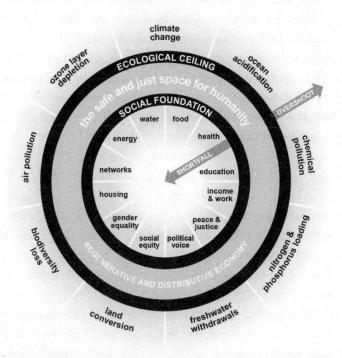

The Doughnut

The inner ring of the doughnut is the social foundation. It represents a sufficiency of the basics of life, such as food, clean water, sanitation, energy, education, healthcare, housing, income and social networks, accompanied by gender equality, peace, justice, democracy and social equity. It is composed, in other words, of the minimum welfare standards established by the UN's Sustainable Development Goals.[17] The hole in the middle represents deprivation: a hole into which no one should have to fall.

The outer ring consists of the Earth's environmental limits – the planetary boundaries identified by the team of scientists led by Johan Rockström and Will Steffen.[18] These include climate change, ozone depletion, nutrient and chemical pollution, freshwater use, the acidification of the oceans, the loss of the diversity and abundance of life, and the destruction of habitats. The aim of the economy should be to bring everyone into the doughnut, which represents the 'ecologically safe and socially just space' for humanity.

Currently, economic life transgresses both limits. Billions of people live below the social foundation, deprived of sufficient food, healthcare, energy, housing, peace, gender equality or political voice. Man-made climate change, the destruction of the biosphere, and water pollution by fertilisers extend far beyond the planetary boundaries.

Bringing economic life into the doughnut means ceasing to leave social and environmental outcomes to chance – ceasing, in other words, to imagine that the magic of the markets will somehow sort it all out. Patently, it has failed to do so. Despite decades of economic growth – the fairy dust that was supposed to make all the bad stuff disappear – the environmental indicators are worse than ever and deteriorating rapidly, while the concentration of wealth in many parts of the world accelerates, leaving the poor in squalor while the rich wallow in fantastic luxury. It turns out that treating the living planet, the core economy, the commons, energy, materials, and most of the world's people as white space on the map, then praying for the divine intervention of the invisible hand and hoping for the best, does not succeed. Who knew?

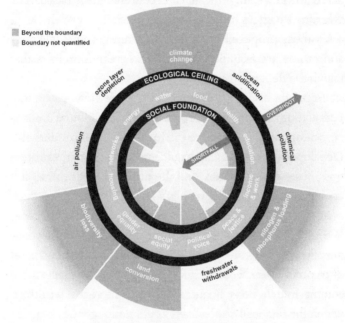

The state in which we find ourselves

Raworth asks us to be agnostic about growth: instead of 'economies that need to grow, whether or not they make us thrive', we need economies that allow us to thrive 'whether or not they grow'. Alongside measures of the kind I discuss in Chapter 6, she proposes shifting taxation from labour to the use of non-renewable resources, and reinforcing this incentive with subsidies for renewable energy and resource efficiency. Economic design should stimulate circular rather than linear production, seeking to produce no waste in the manufacturing process and to create durable products whose components can be reused.

To break the growth hegemony, we need new metrics: measures of well-being rather than expansion. Such 'living metrics' involve monitoring the human, social, ecological and cultural wealth on which all economic life is based. The Genuine Progress Indicator and the Sustainable Well-Being assessment proposed by Robert Costanza, Gar Alperovitz and others are examples of efforts to create measures that match the demands of our age.[19]

We might also need new money. As the New Economics Foundation explains in its report 'Energising Money', monetary design helps determine the form that commerce takes.[20] Developing new currencies could encourage both the protection of the gifts of nature and the distribution of the wealth arising from them. Were money to be tied to resources, such as energy (one proposal is for a currency backed by kilowatt hours), it could help stimulate a transition to a low-use economy. Money anchored to productive value – such as a basket of commodities – would reduce the incentive to exhaust those commodities to boost financial returns. The virtual wealth on which the financial sector feeds could no longer be detached from the real wealth on which all of us survive and thrive.

Black Hole

So how might any of this be implemented? It seems to me that a necessary (though insufficient) step is to take control of public budgets.

Most of the money governments spend is provided by us in tax. But once we have surrendered it, we lose all sense of ownership. Public budgeting is experienced in many parts of the world as state-sponsored robbery. Money is siphoned into projects that are of great benefit to the friends of those in government. It is delivered disproportionately to favoured places (such as the metropolitan centre, or narrowly contested constituencies that the ruling party may wish to acquire), while bypassing other places, including those in greatest need.

In most nations, budgetary decision-making occupies the entire spectrum of legitimacy, ranging from necessary spending, to the pork-barrel project, to clientelism, to outright corruption. Governments too often take the funds that belong to all of us and use them against us, advancing their power at our expense.

In countries without tight controls on campaign finance, the very rich give money to political parties and receive in return public funding, tax concessions, policies and contracts worth many times what they spend. Fossil fuel and electricity companies receive government handouts that are both regressive and environmentally destructive. An opaque budgetary system tends in all cases to favour powerful interests.

This fuels the libertarian demand that we should stop paying taxes. But, given that there are general social benefits that only governments can provide, and given that inequality and exclusion cannot be sensibly addressed without a redistribution of wealth through taxation and public investment, the more appropriate solution is for citizens to exercise intelligible control over the budgeting process.

This might sound expensive and cumbersome, and in some respects it is. But it is much less expensive and cumbersome than the daily spending on behalf of special interests, and the distortion of public infrastructure, subsidy and service provision to meet their needs. What I am calling for is participatory budgeting.

Owning the System

The practice began in the Brazilian city of Porto Alegre in 1989. It has since spread to hundreds of municipalities across the Americas, and in Asia, the Middle East, Africa and Europe, though the great majority of the world's population still languishes under the old system.

While every participatory system is, and should be, slightly different, the methods developed in Porto Alegre provide a basic template. About 20 per cent of the municipal budget – the portion devoted to infrastructure – is allocated by the people.[21] This is a good start, as infrastructure is the item most often captured by corrupt interests; but the aim should be to expand this proportion as the method develops.

The process begins with public meetings that are used to review the previous year's budget and elect local representatives to the new budget council. Working with the people of their districts, these representatives agree local priorities, which are then submitted to the budget council. The council weights the distribution of money according to local levels of poverty and lack of infrastructure. In Porto Alegre, around 50,000 people are typically involved in the development of a budget.

It works. Brazilian cities with participatory budgets have experienced sharper declines in infant mortality and better healthcare and sanitation than those using traditional budgeting.[22] The number of clinics, schools and nursery places in poor areas increases; water supply improves; rivers are cleaned up; poverty declines faster than elsewhere. The poor and their problems can no longer be ignored.

Local gangs and mafias lose their power, as people have other means of securing social protection. The exchange of favours and corrupt practices declines. The language of government changes, allowing anyone to understand the issues at stake and the means by which decisions are made. Good infrastructure comes to be seen by citizens as a right, rather than as a favour to be handed down from on high.

It seems to change the way people see themselves: as powerful citizens, embedded in politics, rather than as docile recipients. As one woman involved in New York's small-scale experiments explained, 'When I went to my first assembly of participatory budgeting, it was the first time in a while, probably ever in my adult life, that I was like "this is democracy. This just feels like democracy, and this is the way decisions should be made in the city."'[23] People perceive that both the system of decision-making and the place in which they live belong to them. Participatory budgeting is, I feel, an essential component of a politics of belonging.

To some extent, it addresses the issues identified by Christopher Achen and Larry Bartels that I mentioned in Chapter 5: namely, that most people possess scarcely any useful information about policies and their implications, and have little desire to improve their state of knowledge.[24] In Porto Alegre it has led to a situation that many politicians consider impossible: large numbers of people demanding that the city council raise their taxes.[25] When you control the budget, you can see what the point of public investment is.

Scaling Up

Exercising control over part of the municipal budget is not enough. The challenge is to find ways to extend the process in two directions: to allow citizens to determine a greater portion of local budgets, and to introduce participatory budgeting at the state and national levels.

The second of these tasks is inherently difficult, as a result of the size of the population that national budgets affect. Democracy becomes fainter as scale increases. The larger the scale of any form of politics, the harder it is to ensure that popular control remains a live proposition.

This problem can be partly solved by devolving as many budgetary powers as possible to the local level. In many nations, central governments retain inordinate control over money that is spent locally. A fundamental principle of a politics of belonging should be that powers and responsibilities are handed to the smallest political unit that can reasonably discharge them. This principle, known as subsidiarity, is widely accepted in theory, but seldom deployed in practice.

Raising the scale of the model means recruiting sympathetic governments that are prepared to start experimenting. It also means replacing governments that try to block such measures. Once we begin to gain control of the budgets that belong to us, our engagement with public investment is likely to proliferate into ever bigger questions: What is the economy for? Who does it serve? What does it ignore? How could it be better designed? In seeking answers, we are drawn almost inexorably towards the principles Raworth identifies: to meet the needs of all within the means of the planet. Her reframing of the economy allows us to see what we were unable to see before.

These questions are too important to be left to economists alone. The answers should belong to all of us.

8

Our Politics

There is a fairly consistent rule in politics: the more rotten a political system is, the more fervently it is admired. Perhaps the most accountable and responsive national democracy is Switzerland's. It is flawed but, as I will explain later in this chapter, less flawed than the rest. As a result, it is used as a ghastly warning of what could happen if – God help us – citizens are granted a greater role in politics.

The least accountable political system among rich nations that purport to be democracies belongs to the United States. A fabulous list of excuses and devices is used to prevent millions of adults, many of whom happen to be poor and black, from exercising their votes. A winner-take-all electoral structure deprives much of the population of effective representation. The president's ability to sign executive orders, to veto bills, to invoke emergency powers and to launch nuclear missiles without legislative authority[1] grants him, in some respects, almost autocratic powers.

Preposterous barriers to entry – massive lists of signatures and tight filing deadlines – are erected to deter parties other than the Democrats and Republicans from competing in elections.[2] Having secured a political duopoly, these parties concentrate power to an extent unknown in comparable nations. Their members exist to send them money, and not much else. Oh, and the entire political system is for sale.

The Pollution Paradox

An analysis by US political scientists found an almost perfect linear relationship, across thirty-two years, between the money available to Congressional candidates and their share of the vote.[3] Those who collect and spend the most money win, while those with the least lose, in almost all cases. In other words, this is not democracy, but plutocracy.

The same study shows that corporations and the very rich spend their money almost exclusively on politics that favours their interests – less taxation of the rich, less redistribution, less protection for people and planet. 'Essentially no major American corporations or members of the Forbes 400 support union drives or politicians like Vermont Senator Bernie Sanders.'[4] To the layperson, this is unsurprising. But so determined are political pundits to justify the US system that these findings were received with amazement.

Overt political spending by the patrimonial elite is supplemented by truckloads of dark money: the undisclosed funding of organisations involved in public advocacy. As I mentioned in Chapter 2, hundreds of groups purporting to be either independent think tanks or grassroots campaigns were founded and financed by billionaires and corporations.[5] Few people would see a tobacco company as a credible source on public health, a coal company as a neutral commentator on climate change, or a billionaire as a disinterested observer of taxes on the very rich. To advance their political interests, such companies and people must pay others to speak on their behalf. Most of the misinformation machines they fund qualify for tax exemptions, as if their purposes were charitable. Staff from these organisations now run much of the Trump administration.[6]

One result of this funding is what I call the Pollution Paradox. The dirtiest companies must spend the most on politics if they are not to be regulated out of existence, so politics comes to be dominated by the dirtiest companies. The paradox applies across the board. Banks designing dodgy financial instruments; pharmaceutical companies selling outdated drugs at inflated prices; gambling companies seeking to stifle controls; food companies selling obesogenic junk: all have an enhanced incentive to buy political space, as all, in a functioning democracy, would find themselves under pressure. Their spending crowds out less damaging interests, and captures the system.

Plutocracy Tempered by Scandal

In the 10th Federalist Paper, written in 1787, James Madison argued that large republics were better insulated from corruption than small, or 'pure' democracies, as the greater number of citizens would make it 'more difficult for unworthy candidates to practice with success the vicious arts by which elections are too often carried'.[7] A large electorate would protect the system against oppressive interest groups. Politics practised on a grand scale would be more likely to select people of 'enlightened views and virtuous sentiments'. He envisaged the constitution of the United States as achieving representation tempered by competition between factions.

Instead, the United States now suffers the worst of both worlds: a large electorate dominated by a tiny faction. Instead of republics being governed, as Madison feared, by 'the secret wishes of an unjust and interested majority', they are beholden to the wishes of an unjust and interested minority. What Madison could not have foreseen was the extent to which unconstrained campaign finance and a sophisticated lobbying industry would come to dominate an entire nation, regardless of its size.

Rather than representation tempered by competition between factions, the political constitution of the United States is plutocracy tempered by scandal. Now, however, scandal has lost its force: the daily revelations of Donald Trump's excesses before the 2016 presidential election appear only to have strengthened his candidacy.

Just as Raskolnikov's mother, in *Crime and Punishment*, once she begins to suspect that he is an axe murderer, reflexively praises her son's many qualities to everyone who will listen, so the political, media and academic establishments glorify the US political system as a temporal paradise. Its characteristics become almost sacred: those who challenge this cesspool of corruption are not just unpatriotic, but anti-democratic.

Noble Rot

The second-worst dispensation in the rich, ostensibly democratic nations is that of the United Kingdom. Here, there are limits on campaign spending, but no limits on the money that any one donor can give. As a result, to an extent greater even than in the United States, a few very rich people or corporations can exercise stupendous unearned political power.

These political rentiers can buy their way into parliament. British party leaders insist that there is no causal relationship between donations and appointments to the upper chamber of the Westminster parliament, the House of Lords. But a study by researchers at Oxford University found that the statistical probability of this being true is 'approximately equivalent to entering the National Lottery and winning the jackpot five times in a row'.[8]

Our first-past-the-post electoral system creates two classes of voters: the majority, who live in constituencies in which power is unlikely to change hands, and can therefore be safely ignored, and a minority (reckoned at 800,000 out of 45 million electors)[9] of floating voters in marginal constituencies, who must be courted and flattered and assuaged with all the resources at parties' disposal. It would be a more honest arrangement if the 44.2 million remnant voters were excluded from the electoral roll: for all the weight given to their views, they might as well be.

I could go on, but you get the general idea. As a result of these evident deficiencies, the political structure of the United Kingdom is attended by dewy-eyed eulogies, generally involving the words 'time-honoured', 'long-established' and 'immutable', as if these were commendations. If I have overemphasised the politics of these two nations in this book, it is not only because theirs are the systems with which I am most familiar, but also because they fail so spectacularly to meet basic democratic standards.

While these are extreme examples, there is no nation on Earth that has embraced the full potential of democratic innovation, new thinking and new technologies. Every polity could be improved, by drawing both on the practices of other nations and on ideas yet to be realised anywhere. In almost every nation, political systems seem remote from our lives. They seldom appear to respond to us or belong to us.

The Protective State

Before exploring the means by which representative democracy could be improved, we should ask ourselves whether we want to improve it. In other words, is it worth saving? It is plainly a system that lends itself to abuse and corruption, and that has often been used to amplify the control of those who are already powerful while suppressing those who are not. So why do we grant power to representatives to act in our name, rather than exercising it directly? Why do we bother with remote authority? Is self-government, as individuals or as members of freely formed communities, not the only true form of democracy?

To answer this question, picture a perfect republic of unarmed black commoners living on their own land, in the absence of all external authority or coercion, next to a perfect republic of well-armed white racists. What do you think is likely to happen? People's loyalty to the members of their own community might be inviolable. But that loyalty is often defined by opposition to another group. When one community regards the members of another as inferior, even subhuman, all ethical constraints fall away. In the ensuing struggle for resources, the winning communities, or their leaders, acquire power. In the absence of government, powerful elites are even more dangerous to the common welfare than they are where the writ of government runs. One of the terms we use for them is warlord.

It is true that our rights and freedoms are often threatened by the state. But how do we defend them in the absence of the state? We would need to find the means not only of resolving conflict with our neighbours, but also of protecting ourselves from the might of people as yet unknown to us. We would need to codify our rights and freedoms and ensure they were respected by others. We would need to discover a common method for protecting them, for preventing violence and theft, and negotiating a balance between our interests and other people's: an arrangement known as the rule of law. In other words, if government ceased to exist, we would need to reinvent it.

The state – partial, flawed and often oppressive as it is – is all that stands between us and the unmediated power of money and weapons. This, after all, is why billionaires and corporations seek to dismantle some of its core functions: the protection of people and the natural world, the redistribution of wealth, the creation of a social safety net and the supply of free, universal public services. Of course, they also seek to capture what remains of the state and use it as a means of enhancing their power. Our task is not to dissolve the state they have corrupted, but to wrest it back from them.

Only the state is big enough to defend us from our common threats.

Consenting Adults

We need a common authority – a government – but we need to bring it within public control, to ensure it belongs to all citizens equally, rather than belonging to a small circle. Democratic power should be grounded in actual choice and consent, rather than in the imagined permission that political systems presumptuously grant themselves. Just as we should in the field of economics, the citizens of a nation should ask themselves a set of fundamental questions: What is politics for? What is it supposed to deliver? What is our role within it? We the people should determine the principles that govern our politics. They should belong to us from the beginning. There is a democratic means of achieving this: a constitutional convention.

What this means is a meeting whose purpose is to identify a set of governing principles and then put them to the vote. While the need is most urgent in countries without a clearly codified constitution (there are just four: the United Kingdom, Israel, New Zealand and Saudi Arabia), the process is useful everywhere. Perhaps every nation should run a constitutional convention once every twenty years, to take stock of its political system, consider new means of enriching democracy, and rectify systemic failings.

Stuart White, who teaches politics at Oxford University, argues that conventions should mostly consist of people who do not already have a formal role in politics.[10] Professional politicians, he reasons, have a vested interest in the status quo. Their positions could be threatened by constitutional change.

So how should members of the convention be chosen? When Iceland created a convention in the wake of the Great Crash, they were elected from people who put themselves forward. The result was an unrepresentative group of citizens: most of them were highly educated. To stand for election, you need plenty of confidence, time and social energy. These obstacles disqualify much of the population.

White argues instead for a process known as sortition: choosing most delegates by lot. The process would not be entirely random, as the population would first be sorted by social category, such as gender, ethnicity, class, age and religion. The aim would be to represent the character of the population as closely as possible: if half the population is female, half the delegates should be. Not everyone will accept the invitation: replacements should also be chosen by lot.

There is an argument for allowing some politicians to join, to ensure that parliament accepts the outcomes. When Ireland held a constitutional convention, two-thirds of the delegates were chosen by sortition and the remainder were politicians. The politicians championed the convention's recommendations in parliament. This might explain why several of the recommendations of the Irish convention were adopted by the government (in one case after a public referendum),[11] while the results of the Icelandic convention were dumped.

Is a randomly selected group of citizens equipped to make such important decisions? The controversial 'Diversity Trumps Ability' theorem proposes that a wide range of life experience is a more useful asset than expertise: a group of citizens from starkly different backgrounds tends to produce a wider range of possible solutions than a group of qualified experts could, including ideas that might have been considered unthinkable by people with specialist training.[12] An international study of citizens' assemblies offers possible support to this theorem.[13]

The professor of politics, Alan Renwick, suggests that the best method is the one used by assemblies in British Columbia and Ontario.[14] In the first phase, expert tutors arrived, often from other parts of the world, to explain the issues to the convention's members. In the second phase, the delegates travelled to public meetings around their provinces and took written submissions from other citizens. In the third phase, helped by facilitators who ensured that every voice was heard, they worked out what to do.

A citizens' convention could be asked by parliament or government to consider certain questions. But, Stuart White reasons, it should be able to change those questions, ignore them, or add to them. In other words, it should be allowed to set its own agenda. We should also have the power, through a petition that attracts a certain number of signatures, to request a convention, perhaps to discuss particular issues, without waiting for parliament to propose one. Citizens' conventions would refer their decisions directly to the people in a referendum, whose authority would be final: parliament would be obliged to implement them.

Political Lottery

If sortition is good enough for a constitutional convention, why should it not replace elections to parliaments? Should our representatives not be chosen by lot, as they were in ancient Athens? This, enthusiasts argue, would prevent systemic corruption and the capture of parliament by powerful interests. It would ensure that parliament was composed of a broad range of citizens, rather than the well-connected and prosperous people the current process favours. But there are some crucial differences between a parliament and a convention.

While the delegates to a constitutional convention might spend one weekend a month, for a year or so, in meetings, parliament sits on most working days, as the volume of business demands. A good parliamentarian returns home with a sack-load of bills and research papers to read and letters to answer. What incentive do randomly chosen citizens have to sustain this workload, week in, week out? How would they be held accountable to their constituents? If their prospects of re-election do not depend on their performance, where is the incentive to engage in the boring and often dispiriting business of the constituency?

Perhaps most dangerously, in trying to comprehend the vast range of issues a parliament considers, the random representatives would depend on a civil service that is permanently established. The civil servants' institutional power – their knowledge of the system, their political and social connections – would be vastly greater than that of the representatives. In seeking to return power to the people, we would hand it instead to the bureaucracy.

There may be an argument for some sortition. If, for example, a quarter of a parliament's members were chosen by lot, they could add to its social and cognitive mix. One proposal suggests that every vote not cast in an election should be considered a vote for sortition.[15] In other words, the percentage of representatives in a parliament who are chosen by election should be the same as the percentage of people who vote, and the remainder should be selected randomly. This is the kind of idea that could be considered by a constitutional convention.

Sense of Proportion

Assuming that elections to parliaments are to continue, as I believe they must, they should be conducted as fairly as possible. If that seems painfully obvious, we should remind ourselves that most systems operate on no such principle. In many of them, the majority of votes might as well not have been cast, as they make no contribution to the eventual result. This might be representative democracy, but it represents only a minority of the population.

Dozens of possible voting methods have been devised, ranging from the imperfect to the abysmal. I will not bore you by cataloguing them; instead I will discuss the one I like best. While all electoral arrangements have disadvantages, it seems to me that the least flawed is the form of proportional representation known as the Single Transferable Vote (STV).

Proportional representation means that the number of seats allocated to a party in a parliament or congress should reflect the number of votes cast. If you think this sounds fair, you differ in this respect from many of the world's politicians, who go to great lengths to justify the systems under which they were elected, using ingenious rhetorical devices.

Of the various forms of proportional representation, STV wins because, while it is directly proportional, it also sustains a sense of local attachment. Voters choose their representatives by name from geographical constituencies, rather than voting for a general list of candidates over which political parties retain control. Constituencies tend to be large, however, and each returns several members to the parliament or congress.

Unlike many other proposed systems, STV possesses a crucial political quality: simplicity. Voters write numbers on the ballot paper beside the names of the candidates they favour, in order of preference. If their first choice of candidate already has sufficient votes, or has no chance of election, their vote is switched during the count to their second choice.

The STV system ensures that almost everyone has a member for whom they voted and to whom they can turn in the expectation of a sympathetic hearing, rather than the pantomime of interest with which a hostile representative will receive them. To appeal to as wide a group of voters in a constituency as possible, parties have an incentive to field a broad slate of candidates. This is likely to boost the numbers of women, people of colour and others who tend to be under-represented in political life.[16]

A common criticism of proportional representation, particularly the single transferable vote, is that it creates governing coalitions in which small parties have excessive influence. In other words, the proportional method produces disproportionate governments (an example is the power of extremist parties in Israel). This is a real danger, though generally a transitory one. By contrast, the disproportionate influence of large parties in majoritarian systems, in some cases elected by a quarter or less of the adult population, can persist indefinitely.

A system in which almost every vote counts and almost every voice can find a fair hearing during the electoral term is a system likely to build engagement, trust and belonging. But the electoral process alone does not guarantee that politics works.

Democracy Is Cheap

If no one's vote is to count for more than any other, no one's money should either. No voting system, without constraints on campaign finance, can prevent the very rich from buying the policies and even the election results they want. Fair politics means fair funding. This, I believe, is another essential element of a politics of belonging.

It is so easy to devise an equitable political funding method that, as soon as you begin to think about it, you realise that the problem is political, not logistical. Understandably, political incumbents seek to resist proposals that would serve everyone but themselves and their donors. However obvious the necessary reform may be, these people will fight it by all possible means. They own the system: why would they wish to relinquish it? As with all the suggestions in this book, the old dispensation will be swept away only when our demands for a better one are transformed into a determined political campaign with a clear and simple message around which we mobilise, using techniques of the kind described in the next chapter.

Here is an example of a fair political funding system. Every party or independent candidate would be entitled to charge the same small fee for membership (independents would be encouraged to form a supporters' club) – perhaps $20, £20, or its equivalent in other currencies. This would be matched by the state, on a fixed multiple. Any other political funding of parties and candidates, whether spent by the parties and candidates themselves or by others on their behalf, would be illegal. The arrangement would be simple, transparent and entirely dependent on the enthusiasm politicians could muster. They would have a powerful incentive to re-engage with voters to raise their membership. The funding of referendums is even simpler: the state should provide an equal amount for those campaigning on each side of the question.

This issue has been supremely complicated in the United States by perverse judicial rulings: a constitutional amendment would be required to negate them. Elsewhere, the only sustained objection I have seen to such proposals is that they would cost too much. In the United Kingdom, the system I propose would require around £50 million of public spending for a general election. That represents scarcely a rounding error in national accounts.

The cost of the current system is the destruction of democracy in anything but name: financial crises, caused by the ability of the financial sector to buy its way out of democratic constraints; the environmental crisis, exacerbated by the political power that destructive industries have purchased; the wages crisis and the collapse of working conditions, caused by the freedom to exploit that employers have purchased; and innumerable bad, destructive and irrational policies, arising from the generalised corruption of politics, as well as the rise of an extremist anti-politics in response to a broken and unresponsive system. In other words, it runs into many billions. It runs beyond billions, into costs that money alone cannot represent.

Regulating the dark-money network is a little harder. There is nothing wrong in principle with external political advocacy: in fact, it is essential to effective democratic politics. There are two features that a fair system would suppress. The first is the inordinate power of the very rich, who can buy an infrastructure of persuasion not available to others. The second is the secrecy and deception they employ in seeking to hide their spending and persuade us that the groups they have purchased are independent and self-organised.

There is no complete solution. The first step is for governments to stop treating such organisations as charities: in other words, to cease exempting them from tax and granting them associated privileges. The second is to insist that any organisation involved in public advocacy publicly declares all donations of, say, $1,000 or more. The third is that, when people from advocacy groups appear in the media, the media organisation, to fulfil legal standards of accountability and transparency, should mention any of the group's financial interests that are relevant to the discussion. In other words, the rule would be similar to those that apply in parliaments, where members must reveal any financial interests pertinent to the debates they join.

Blunt Instrument

Even if representative democracy is reformed along these lines, it cannot by itself meet the complexity and range of our needs: it is too clumsy a method to attend to the level of detail demanded by good governance in the twenty-first century. There is no contradiction between an accountable representative system and a rich culture of participation. In fact, the one depends upon the other. At present, in most nations, we have neither.

It is a paradox of an age dominated by neoliberal thought that, while we are promised the autonomy associated with extreme individualism (which generally turns out to be illusory), the political system has scarcely devolved its powers since the era of ironclad ships and telegrams.

Having won an election, governments claim a mandate for all the policies they can persuade parliaments to adopt, without referring them back to the people on whose behalf they claim to govern. What this means in practice is that they will use parliamentary or congressional majorities to push through some of the promises featured in their manifesto or platform (while conveniently forgetting others), to introduce others that were never mentioned, and to quash counter-proposals, including some that enjoy widespread public support.

If they are challenged on these issues, they point to the election that brought them to office, insisting that it legitimises everything they do until they face the next election, which may be four or five years away. If we do not like the policies they implement, democracy, they argue, permits us to replace them with a government we prefer.

How many times have I been told, 'If you don't like it, why don't you stand for election?' – as if the only valid political role a citizen can play is to become a representative. In the nation to which I belong, of some 60 million, this riposte suggests that only 650 people have a legitimate place in national politics, beyond voting once every five years.

The result is a system that offers us political control so coarse and diffuse that democracy loses all but its crudest meaning. Hundreds of issues are bundled into every election, as a result of which almost none are politically intelligible. A government might be elected (often by a minority of the adult population) principally because of its economic promises, or its position on crime or immigration, but it will use its election to claim support for all the issues in its manifesto – which might include airport development, food safety standards, wage levels, disability benefits, health spending, foreign policy, the right to protest, funding the arts, and weapons procurement – and for anything else it decides to change during its term in office.

These decisions will be imposed on everyone, regardless of their choice at the election, and often regardless of the unpopularity of the particular policies. Without a meaningful opportunity to consider such policies, it is hard for us even to determine our view of them. Excluded from decision-making, we are reduced to passive recipients of whatever distorted account the media chooses to produce. Everything, across the entire term of office, is justified by reference to a single decision made on a single day. A fine-grained democratic control over the decisions affecting our lives is denied to us.

It might have been possible to offer a partial justification for this system when the quill pen was the fastest means of record-taking and the horse was the swiftest means of transport. It is unjustified in the digital era. The idea that any government could meet the needs of a modern nation by ruling without constant feedback, and actual rather than notional consent, is ridiculous. It frustrates the potential offered by current technologies for a democracy worthy of the term. It thwarts our need for a system within which we can belong.

Slanging Match

At present, the people of many nations are trapped in a vicious circle. Disempowered and alienated, they have neither experience of meaningful participation, nor faith that their involvement will lead to political change. Governments are equally suspicious, believing – as they have never witnessed it – that true participation will lead to chaos and disaster.

A well-meaning local councillor might call a meeting to discuss an issue of great importance, such as the funding crisis in local schools, only to find herself being shouted at for two hours about dog shit and parking. This is how disempowered people without either the means or the incentive to engage effectively tend to respond. Politicians then assume that meaningful consultation is pointless, and revert to business as usual.

Something similar happened when people in the United Kingdom were asked to decide whether or not to stay in the European Union. The government threw the biggest possible question at an electorate that had almost no experience of direct democracy. Instead of building towards the decision with a series of small participatory events, such as citizens' juries, in which people might have had a chance to work through the issues together, voters were rushed towards judgement day on a ridiculously short timetable, with no preparation except a series of humongous lies.

After years of being marginalised, disenfranchised and treated like idiots, people recognised that, in many cases for the first time in their lives, they were being offered genuine political power. The question over which they would wield it was a secondary matter: the vote became a proxy for all the issues over which they had been denied real choice. Presented with the options of the status quo or rupture, the only means of exercising that power was to vote for rupture.

Effective participation requires a lively, creative and intelligent political culture; a lively, creative and intelligent political culture requires effective participation. Breaking this impasse in nations whose people have seldom been meaningfully involved in politics will take time, patience and experiments. If participatory democracy is to become more than a slanging match between uninformed people about unrelated issues, it should become a familiar and trusted form of political expression. It should, in other words, look something like the Swiss system.

A Sovereign People

In a survey of forty rich nations, the Organisation for Economic Cooperation and Development found that, on average, 42 per cent of people expressed 'confidence in government'.[17] But in Switzerland, which came first, the rate was 75 per cent. In the seven years since the previous survey, confidence levels had risen there by 12 points, while they had fallen by an average of 3 per cent elsewhere. This is not, of course, a definitive measure of the quality of government: an autocratic state that has invested heavily in propaganda can command the confidence of many of its citizens (Russia, for example, ranks high on the list). But given that national rhetoric in Switzerland tends to be quiet and comparatively modest, this is unlikely to account for its position.

Switzerland is no paradise. Much of its wealth arises from a corrupt and opaque banking sector (a feature it shares with the United Kingdom). Not only are there no limits to political funding or spending, but there is no transparency either: a bizarre and outrageous omission. Its government is politely described as stable, less politely as stale: it is overseen by a federal council of seven members whose political composition has scarcely changed since 1959. The council carves up power between the major parties at the expense of smaller players. (In its favour, it prevents any single faction or person from monopolising control).

What possible reason might Swiss citizens have to vest so much confidence in their public institutions? It is simple: to a greater extent than the people of any other nation, they exercise control over them. The great constitutional question – where should sovereignty reside, in parliament or in the people? – has been decisively resolved in favour of the people.

The people of Switzerland vote in around ten referendums a year, clustered into three or four polling days. Some of these are initiated by parliament, some by citizens. Any law passed by parliament can be challenged by the people. If, within one hundred days, someone can furnish 50,000 signatures from people opposed to the law, the government is obliged to put the question to the country. These referendums are binding: if the people vote against it, the law is struck down. People can also propose amendments to the constitution, if they can gather 100,000 signatures within eighteen months. The federal council might suggest a counter-proposal, which is put to the popular vote at the same time.

These procedures horrify many onlookers. They argue that they are likely to lead to instability (hardly a problem in Switzerland), extremism, the oppression of minorities by majorities, and the rule of ignorance and simplicity.

It is true that some Swiss referendums have approved illiberal measures, such as a ban on the construction of new minarets. Other immoderate proposals, however, such as the expulsion of foreign criminals and an attempt to ban same-sex couples from marrying, have been rejected, while in 2016 a law granting asylum seekers free legal assistance was approved.[18] Here as elsewhere, referendums are likely to reflect (and reveal) the character of the nation, which in the Swiss case is generally conservative.

Rather than fostering extremism, the system tends to encourage caution (sometimes excessive caution) among political parties: they hesitate to introduce disruptive laws for fear of triggering a referendum. While direct democracy might limit innovation by governments, it stimulates innovation by citizens. The impact of the system is to favour the median voter, but people's right to launch referendums allows issues and views that have been marginalised to be brought to the fore.

The overall effect, as the Swiss diplomat Simon Geissbühler reports, is to encourage public engagement with politics, high levels of political information, and reasoned debate.[19] Still more important is the sense of political owner-ship the system fosters: people perceive that government belongs to them. This is how trust in politics is earned.

Of course, the Swiss method could be improved, not least through campaign finance reform. At present, well-funded groups are more likely to be able to raise the necessary signatures than those that struggle to attract big money. There is also an argument, as the campaign group Democracy International proposes, for oversight by a supreme constitutional court, to ensure that referendum decisions do not breach fundamental human rights: this would provide a safeguard against the tyranny of majorities.

The political thinker Peter Emerson argues that instead of being confronted with raw binary decisions, voters in referendums should typically be given a choice of several options. For example, in the UK's referendum on membership of the European Union, voters might have been asked whether they wished to retain full European membership, membership of the European Economic Area (EEA) but not the Union, membership of neither the EU nor the EEA but just the Customs Union, or no relationship at all, in which case trading arrangements would be negotiated through the World Trade Organisation. Because no such choice was presented, everyone knows what the majority voted against; no one knows what it voted for.

While a yes–no referendum treats us like simpletons, by demanding the complete acceptance or complete rejection of an elaborate law or institution, a multiple-choice referendum reveals the complexity of the question, and encourages people to consider the implications of their choice. It obliges the government to offer a detailed explanation of what change would mean.

The Wisdom of Crowds

If referendums were used to address every issue that needed to be resolved, they would quickly lose their power. Turnout would fall to the point at which nations became subject to the tyranny of the politics geek. But smaller questions can still be addressed directly, and digital technology, in principle at least, makes this easier.

The innovation foundation Nesta warns that there are no quick or cheap digital fixes. The reality of digital democracy has so far 'not lived up to early hopes and expectations': it has tended 'to involve fairly small and unrepresentative numbers of citizens'.[20] But there are a few models that point to how it could develop.

For example, vTaiwan is an online consultation tool that seeks to resolve narrow but tricky issues.[21] People meet on an online forum, share facts about the issue (which are checked by facilitators), and exchange views. Their recommendations are then passed to the Taiwanese government. I would hesitate to call it democracy: it looks more like the pooling of expertise among a large crowd of people with specialist knowledge. But it has improved the quality and speed of decision-making. In one case (what to do about online sales of alcohol) it produced a solution to a problem parliament had been unable to resolve.

The chamber of deputies (the lower house of Congress) in Brazil has taken the process further. It crowdsourced 30 per cent of its Youth Bill from young people through an electronic portal.[22] Much of its Internet Civil Rights Bill was also supplied by online citizens. Again, it seems to have improved the range of ideas and quality of political debate, but again the process drew on a small subsection of society.

The best example of online democracy so far is the scheme developed in Reykjavík to allow people to propose ideas for improving the city and influence the infrastructure budget.

So far, astonishingly, 70,000 of the city's 120,000 people have taken part.[23]

Anyone can propose an improvement; anyone can vote for or against it. The fifteen most popular ideas each month are passed to the city council to consider. During the first six years of the programme, 1,000 ideas were submitted, of which over 200 were adopted. The result seems to have been a major enhancement of both civic life and the city's amenities.

Why does it work so well? Partly because the ideas are reviewed every month: the rapid feedback enhances public trust. And partly because the city authorities provide clear and reasoned explanations for their decisions, including their rejection of proposals. People can see that they are not throwing their ideas into the void.

Digital democracy is no magic wand. It risks empowering one group (typically tech-savvy young men) at the expense of others. It is vulnerable to hacking by money and undemocratic power. Online forums are placeless. Used well, they can enhance our sense of belonging (this seems to be the case in Reykjavík); used badly, they could undermine it. Digital engagement should be seen as a supplement to real life, not a substitute for it.

New technologies could expand its potential. For example, as natural language processing improves, it could be used to analyse vast consultations. Algorithms seek out key words and syntax, gaining a sense of the balance of opinion. They also search for unusual vocabulary and sentence forms that, as artificial intelligence improves, might allow them to identify and highlight original thinking. These are tasks that, when many thousands of people respond, civil servants could not perform except at monumental expense. This might enable the Reykjavík model to be scaled up to allow meaningful mass participation in national decisions.

The blockchain ledger (the technology used to verify the owners of Bitcoin) could be used to confirm online identities, and potentially votes, preventing fraud, trolling and botswarming (using hundreds of fake accounts to create the impression that an idea has popular support). Its potential to transform democracy has been wildly exaggerated by some people, however,[24] who see it as a means of dispensing with government altogether, replacing public provision with online market transactions: the neoliberal fantasy taken to its ultimate conclusion.[25] Even lesser roles for the blockchain ledger might potentially be co-opted, as those with the most computing power could come to control the verification process. We cannot expect miracles from digital technologies, but we can, when they are used well, expect improvements.

Lighting a Candle

The most obvious application of digital technologies is to provide us with the information we need to make intelligent political choices. When we vote, or participate in any other way, we should do so as informed and thoughtful citizens, rather than arriving at the polling station in a haze of ignorance and confusion and stabbing our pencils at a name we vaguely recognise while muttering, 'They're all as bad as each other.'

Political understanding is made as hard as humanly possible by the billionaire press, the creeping influence of purchased online content, the dark-money network of bogus think tanks, and all the other purveyors of fake news and 'alternative facts'. Our inherent bias and ignorance are reinforced by the closed circles of opinion we consult and the personalisation of online news (the filter bubble). Few people set out to find correctives to their mistaken beliefs; even fewer are likely to succeed.

We might not take it up, but we should at least have a chance to inform ourselves better. One of the democratic duties of governments is to assist us by spreading objective information. A good start would be to copy Germany and Switzerland.

Germany's Federal Agency for Civic Education has 200 staff.[26] It publishes books, pamphlets, materials for schools, and webpages about the key political issues of the day, and organises film and theatre festivals, study tours and competitions. It runs an online service called Wahl-O-Mat, consulted many millions of times during elections, that presents a list of political statements to the competing parties and asks them to say whether they agree, disagree or have no position on them.[27] The same questionnaire is then published. Voters can supply their own answers, and rank the importance of the issues. The website then compares their answers to those of the parties, to show people which party best matches their positions.

Switzerland takes this a step further. Its Smartvote platform allows electors to compare their positions not only with the parties but also with the candidates in their constituencies, generating a graphic showing where they stand in relation to those who wish to represent them.[28] This could, of course, reinforce bias, though it might also prompt people to question their customary votes. In either case, it helps voters to cross a crucial barrier: seeing themselves as political agents who can exercise meaningful choice, rather than as people to whom politics is done.

Global Democracy

This book's implicit assumption, so far, is that the nation-state is the primary focus of political life. But one of the crises we confront is that power has leaked out of national institutions and into global forums, where it can no longer be held to account.

Power crosses national borders freely, but democracy stops at the boarding gate. Transnational corporations push nation-states into destructive competition, demanding, under the threat of relocating, lower rates of corporation tax, weaker employment and environmental rules, and the suppression of trade unions. There are no effective global mechanisms for constraining their power and holding them to account. Trade treaties are drafted behind closed doors, in a process dominated by corporations and subject to no direct democratic oversight.

The IMF, the World Bank and the UN Security Council are controlled by a minority of nations (the United States, uniquely, has veto powers over all three), but their writ extends globally. The IMF and the World Bank, controlled by the rich, operate mostly in poorer nations, imposing austerity and deregulation on their governments. Bodies that are ostensibly controlled by all governments, such as the World Trade Organisation and the United Nations General Assembly, operate entirely on the basis of presumed consent.

The member-states seldom refer the positions they take in these forums to their people. As power is shifted to the global level, we are disenfranchised accordingly.

There are two possible responses. One is to seek to repatriate global power; the other is to seek to democratise it.

There are plenty of issues that can be resolved only globally. For example, the greatest threat we face, climate breakdown, requires international action. Debt between nations, the balance of trade, nuclear proliferation, the manufacture and sale of illegal weapons, war, international crime, the shipment of toxic waste, the traffic of endangered wildlife, pollution and overfishing of the oceans: none of these can be addressed only within national borders.

Plainly, the principle of subsidiarity should operate here: only issues that nation-states cannot handle should be determined at the global level. But to what extent could global powers be repatriated? On some issues, states could act unilaterally. For example, they could simply refuse to accept instructions from the IMF or the European Central Bank when these bodies insist that governments cripple their economies, destroy their public services and throw millions out of work on behalf of the private banking industry. If this means defaulting on their unpayable debts or falling out of the Eurozone, it might be judged a price worth paying. If enough states followed suit, the political crisis would shift from them to the IMF or the ECB, whose credibility would crumble as states stopped responding to their diktats.

A general and systemic repatriation of powers to nation-states can come about by two means: the unplanned breakdown of the global order (this is likely to be either accomplished or accompanied by war, and should be feared more than it is welcomed), or global agreement. I hope you have spotted the paradox: a peaceful withdrawal from political globalisation requires political globalisation. This is not to say it cannot be done, when enough governments – including the most powerful – support this approach. It is to say that it would be a long and difficult process.

For the reasons I have explained, not all powers can or should be repatriated. But global bodies have no more right than any others to operate without explicit public consent.

In a previous book, *The Age of Consent*, I proposed some means by which global governance could be made both more democratic and more responsive to the will of the world's people.[29] I argued that the UN Security Council should be scrapped, and its powers vested in a reformulated UN General Assembly. This would be democratised by means of weighted voting: nations' votes would increase according to both the size of their populations and their positions on a global democracy index.

The World Trade Organisation should be replaced by a new body – a Fair Trade Organisation – which, instead of subjecting all nations, regardless of their power and wealth, to the same set of global rules, allows poorer nations to protect their infant industries from foreign competition until they are strong enough to fend for themselves (this is the path to prosperity that most rich nations followed). This would ensure that companies operating between nations would be subject to mandatory fair trade rules, losing their licence to trade if they exploited workers or damaged the living world. (In other words, it would set minimum standards for trade, rather than the maximum standards now imposed by global treaties).

The World Bank and the IMF, which are governed without a semblance of democracy and cause more crises than they solve, should be replaced by a body charged with preventing excessive trade surpluses and deficits from forming, and therefore international debt from accumulating. Overseeing all these institutions and holding them to account, I propose a directly elected world parliament.

Given where power now lies, these are vastly ambitious suggestions (vastly ambitious, of course, is what we need to be). They also face certain inherent difficulties, the most obvious of which is that democracy is diluted with increasing scale. I would argue that a weak and remote democracy is better than no democracy at all, especially if it were supplemented by new participatory techniques.

A New Order?

To what extent do we still need nation-states? We tend to imagine that they have always existed and always will, but they are a recent phenomenon, and could be a temporary one. A study by the journalist Debora MacKenzie explains that, before the late eighteenth century, there were no clear national boundaries, and no border checks.[30] Even in the nineteenth century, many Europeans could not name the nation to which they belonged. The locus of attachment for most people was their village or town. The discrete nation-state developed in response to rising industrial and social complexity. National identities typically had to be invented, with the help of flags, anthems, ideologies, revised histories and linguistic conformity.

Do nation-states enhance the general welfare of humankind, or impede it? Some have suppressed civil conflict, others have exacerbated it. MacKenzie proposes that the crucial factor is the extent to which the various cultural and ethnic groups are included in the national project. She argues that it is not diversity itself that causes civil strife, but the systematic denial of power to particular factions. You can see the results in Iraq, where the US administration, following the 2003 invasion, established a government dominated by Shia, from which Sunnis were largely excluded, and in Syria, where the government is dominated by the Alawite Shia minority, whose interests are favoured at the expense of other groups. In response, the Sunni terrorists Isis/Daesh have sought to create their own state, straddling both nations.

Such conflict, according to the researchers MacKenzie interviewed, is best averted by subsidiarity – the devolution of power to the smallest appropriate unit. This is how Switzerland resolved the crises arising from its ethnic and linguistic diversity. Paradoxically, perhaps, the more autonomy within the nation we possess, the greater is our sense that we belong to it.

Complexity gave rise to the nation-state; further complexity could destroy it. There is a point at which large societies may simply become too complex to run. Perhaps this point has already been reached, which would help to explain our multifaceted crisis.[31] If so, the answer is likely to be a shift in the location of power.

Let us imagine, even if we are not yet ready or willing to act upon it, the end of the large nation-state. Perhaps we could envisage a system whose primary political unit is the city and its hinterland, or the subnational region (the canton in the Swiss model). This authority would then devolve all possible powers to its districts, counties and villages. It would collaborate with other cantons to solve common problems, creating federal forums to resolve certain issues but remaining independent in other respects. The federal forums would delegate still larger issues to a global body, whose scope and powers would be closely defined.

At every level, from the village to the global forum, there would be a directly elected body exercising primacy over both unelected and indirectly elected institutions. Every elected body would be subject to the will of the people, who could challenge or propose legislation through referendums, and suggest and refine ideas in physical or online forums. Everywhere, sovereignty would reside in the people.

By these means, we could perhaps begin to strike a balance between universalism and belonging. Without compromising our fundamental rights, we could reclaim power over the systems that purport to represent us. This is what democracy looks like.

9

Making It Happen

Some of the policies in this book could be implemented immediately. But most of this story cannot be realised without regime change. Unless people and parties supporting a generous, inclusive politics win elections, the hope this book aims to ignite will remain unfulfilled.

Winning elections means not only attracting more votes than your opponents. It also means doing so without abandoning your principles.

To judge by their strategies over the past thirty years, most of the world's social-democratic parties see this as impossible. Winning, they came to believe, required the renunciation of almost everything they had once stood for, and its replacement with the ideology of their opponents. Only when their politics became acceptable to the proprietors of the newspapers and other billionaires, they believed, was electoral success possible. To win, they had to lose. Taking power meant abandoning power; victory required retreat on all fronts.

Losing their principles meant losing the passionate support of their base. As the loyalty of their supporters was replaced by disillusionment, the ambitions of these parties shrank further. As they lost and failed to replace their stories, they had nothing left to say. Their pessimism about radical change became self-fulfilling.

The Promise of Big Organising

This point is illustrated by a remarkable near-miss: the attempt by Senator Bernie Sanders to become the Democratic candidate in the 2016 US presidential election.

When Sanders officially launched his campaign, in May 2015, everything seemed to be against him. Just 3 per cent of the electorate recognised his name. He was treated by much of the media as a marginal and superannuated figure (he was seventy-four), whose politics were so far removed from the Beltway consensus that he could be safely ignored. His programme – the redistribution of income and wealth from the rich to the poor and middle; the break-up of the big banks; radical action on climate change; universal healthcare provided by the state; major restrictions on campaign finance – was considered either laughable or diabolical by the political mainstream. He refused to court major funders, relying instead on small donations from his supporters. Leaked emails later revealed that senior members of the Democratic National Committee, including its chair, plotted to undermine his campaign, going so far as to discuss proposing lines of attack to the media.[1]

By the time the contest was over, he had captured twenty-two states and 46 per cent of the pledged delegates. In other words, he almost won, without compromising his political position. Had he succeeded – well, who knows what would have happened? It was obvious to many at the time, and many more in retrospect, that American voters were craving major change. Hillary Clinton, the continuity candidate who represented everything that had gone wrong with the Democratic Party – its dynastic self-regard, its umbilical relationship with Wall Street, its reliance on big money, its technocratic machine politics and abandonment of principle – could not deliver it. Perhaps only Sanders could have beaten Trump.

So how did this man, dismissed from the outset as a no-hoper, come so close to securing the nomination? Part of the answer is provided in the most encouraging book I have read in years. *Rules for Revolutionaries: How Big Organizing Can Change Everything*, written by two of Sanders's campaigners, Becky Bond and Zack Exley, explains how, with hardly any staff and a tiny initial budget, they built the biggest voter-contact operation ever unleashed in a presidential primary.[2]

Had they known at the beginning of the campaign what they knew by the end, Sanders would have been irresistible. But by the time they stumbled across the strategy that almost won the nomination, it was too late. They see this not as a cause of frustration, but as a source of hope: if the methods they developed are used from the beginning, they could transform the prospects of any campaign for a better world.

The Curse of Small Organising

As the Democrats and similar parties offer ever less to their supporters, they come to expect ever less in return.

Campaigns such as Hillary Clinton's presidential bid begin with the assumption that the key to victory is big money and big data. Big data, in this context, means information about voters, allowing staff to identify those who might swing from one party to another. Treating such electors as the campaign target means shifting ever further towards the positions of your opponents.

As this strategy offers only minimal changes in a few fairly safe areas of policy, the campaign cannot rely on public enthusiasm for its success. Instead, it becomes wholly dependent on paid staff, micromanaging a controlled and technical operation. This, in turn, ensures it becomes ever less ambitious and ever more reliant on big money to pay its staff. This is the curse of what Bond and Exley call 'small organising'.

Transformational change does not happen this way. The great emancipations – from women's suffrage to Civil Rights, to independence from empire and the end of apartheid – came about through the mass mobilisation of citizens. Future political revolutions will follow the same course. Big change requires Big Organising.

Big Organising means starting with major goals: policies commensurate with the scale of the challenges we face. It means pursuing big targets: most of the electorate, rather than a few narrow segments. It means relying on a great mobilisation of volunteers. And it means asking them to make a major commitment: to invest a lot of their time to perform crucial tasks. Paradoxically, Bond and Exley report, the more you ask of people, the more likely they are to come forward: 'far more people are willing to step up if you ask them to do something big to win something big than . . . if you asked them to do something small to win something small'.

Only Connect

The Sanders campaign was a gigantic live experiment. What the experiment revealed – too late to swing the outcome – was that volunteers can fill almost all the positions traditionally reserved for staff. As the method for recruiting and mobilising them was refined, the campaign found that there was almost no limit to what they were prepared to do, as long as the goals and the requests were big enough. By the end of the nomination process, more than 100,000 people had been recruited. Between them, they ran 100,000 events and spoke to 75 million voters. While the Clinton campaign was organising money, the Sanders campaign was organising people.

The campaign's key realisation was that voters are not much moved by television ads, direct mail, people waving signs at them on street corners, and automated messages from a robot caller. What brings them round is a conversation with a real person, ideally a person like themselves, rather than a paid persuader. It does not matter whether this conversation is on the telephone or on the doorstep. The deep need for social contact that defines our species can also change our politics.

The Sanders campaign discovered that conversations between volunteers and other citizens – people whose footing in society is, in other words, more or less equal – not only motivate people to vote for a candidate, but can also 'change deeply held attitudes regarding controversial issues such as transgender rights', and that 'those changed attitudes can endure over time'. The advice is beautifully simple: junk the advertising, junk the data, junk the political machine, and talk.

Bernie Sanders's uncompromising messages had inspired people all over the United States to offer their services. The campaign had compiled a vast list of emails, but at first it had no idea what to do with them. The answer emerged after months of trial and error. It was to contact all the volunteers in a particular town or city and ask them to come to a mass meeting (a 'barnstorm'). Only one email was required to organise each meeting; everywhere people turned up in droves.

At these barnstorms, there was no need to explain the issues at length, to educate or motivate people: they already knew why they were there, and just wanted to be put to work. The organisers spelled out the campaign strategy, then asked people to commit, there and then, to hosting phone-banking events, in their homes or in any room they could borrow. Generally, around 10 per cent of the audience would volunteer. These people would then line up at the front of the meeting and announce the date, time and place at which they would run their event, and ask the rest of the audience to sign up to it – not by email, or at a later date, but, again, on the spot.

When people get together to make calls, the campaign discovered, they work harder, enjoy it more, and have more effective conversations with potential voters than if they work alone: the power of connection seems to operate at every level. The volunteers were given access to the campaign's phone-dialler software, contact details for the helpdesk (which was also run by volunteers), training videos, and a script. Then, in front rooms, cafés, offices and public buildings, using their own phones, they would get to work, each talking to around twenty-five people per hour.

The next discovery was that the mass meetings could also be led by unpaid activists: they were just as effective as the salaried staff at organising and mobilising people. As a result, there were no financial or logistical constraints on the number of barnstorms: they proliferated spontaneously all over the country. Altogether, 1,000 were held, of which 650 were run by people who had put themselves forward. Each of them launched several teams of people who, within a few days, were phoning electors in their district. As people realised that there was something meaningful they could do, word spread on social media: thousands came forward in every state.

Radical Trust

The campaign quickly discovered that only a minimum of supervision was required. This does not mean that the volunteers invented their own tasks: the goals and methods and phone scripts were still determined centrally by staff. But it does mean that they could execute the plan with scarcely any oversight. Bond and Exley and their team developed a model they call 'radical trust': delegating the biggest possible tasks to volunteers and leaving them to get on with it. Their aim was to be big rather than perfect; by relinquishing control, they got more done. While occasionally volunteers let them down, they found that most were 'more passionate and driven than any staff could ever be'.

Many of those who came forward were new to campaigning – these people tended to be the most enthusiastic and creative workers.

There were some roles that could not safely be allocated to unpaid activists, such as the national press operation, where a small mistake could have major consequences. But almost anything else could be. Formal training turned out to be unnecessary: a one-page guide and a short video were all that the phone-bank volunteers required. With the clever use of communications software, a few paid staffers could coordinate the work of thousands of volunteers.

Big Organising freed the campaign from the grip of big money. Those who joined the campaign and those they spoke to began to donate. Bernie Sanders raised $230 million from 2.8 million people. Because fundraising became an organic part of the campaign, he had no need to waste a minute of his time listening to the demands of big donors. He could stay true to his principles without worrying about the money.

Reaching Everyone

It could have been bigger. Much bigger. Had they done it all again, Bond and Exley would have advised dispensing with ordinary marketing and using the small pot of money with which the Sanders bid began to put volunteers to work immediately. They would have allowed the volunteers to organise state campaigns long before any staff arrived, to set up their own offices, and to create a leadership structure whose most effective members could then be recruited into the state staff when enough money arrived. Volunteers would have organised barnstorming meetings every week in every neighbourhood, to activate new aspects of the campaign. And they would have had the time and the scope to start a national conversation about the future of America – on every telephone line and doorstep in the Union.

This is perhaps the most exciting discovery: that, had it been activated a few months earlier, the volunteer network could have abandoned all forms of targeting and simply contacted everyone – every adult in the United States of America. By the time his campaign ended, the Bernie Sanders network had developed the capacity to do this, a capacity that would have been mobilised had he won the nomination.

This, the authors contend, is how we 'swamp the influence of big money, corporate media and other establishment players'. However much money the billionaires pour into the campaigns of their favoured candidates, they are unlikely to be able to hire enough staff to contact everyone. And if they do, those staff are unlikely to resemble the people they talk to. A bold, generous, inclusive politics can mobilise volunteer numbers that those who buy their influence could never hope to attract.

What Bond and Exley have given us is not a script, but a template: an idea that can be adapted to any situation; a means of mobilising a rolling and self-generating wave of volunteers whose passion proliferates into ever wider networks. To read their book is to release yourself from the poverty of imagination that has locked us into despair. It is to start imagining how campaigns of any kind – not just to win elections but to win the battle over climate change, or rights for asylum seekers or for universal healthcare – can be transformed. It is to understand how we can mobilise the enthusiasm of the many against the control of the few. And it shows us how a political campaign can belong to everyone who chooses to participate, rather than just a small cadre of professionals.

Point of Contact

Here is a small example of something we could do better, as a result of applying the kind of strategies the Bernie Sanders team pioneered. The most visible expression of dissent is the public demonstration. This, for many campaigns, is their showcase: an opportunity to explain the problems we face, to articulate an alternative, to attract new supporters, and to mobilise them into an effective force for change. A demonstration is often the first point of contact for those who have never been involved in politics before. If it is badly handled, it will also be the last point of contact.

A good demonstration should meet two definitions of the word: it should be a demonstration against the forces we oppose, and a demonstration of the better future we envisage. And it should observe the first two rules of effective campaigning: identify exactly what you are trying to achieve, and ensure that every step you take towards that objective leads to the next step. There are some notable exceptions, but most of those I have attended fail on all counts.

Typically, a march is planned. Great effort and energy is invested in publicising it and organising the logistics. Sometimes, even at short notice, these efforts will succeed in bringing together thousands of people. At this point, the planning disintegrates: having assembled the crowd, the organisers have no idea what to do with it. So they do what they have always done. They stand on a podium and bring on speaker after speaker to ramble at the audience.

Most of these speakers are chosen not for their ability to captivate, inspire or inform a crowd, but because they helped to organise the event or belong to groups represented by the event. The speaking rota is created for their benefit – every subgroup should be given a say – rather than the benefit of the listeners. The speeches range from the inaudible to the ranty, but they have one thing in common: they are always too long. People start to freeze, the kids tug at their parents' hands, the mood deflates.

Then the convener will lead the crowd in a chant. This tends to be either a chant thought up on the spot or one they have been leading for the past twenty years, which may or may not have some vague association with the theme of the protest. The audience will take it up out of duty rather than conviction. Soon, the words die in their mouths. Then, for want of anything better to do, the convener will announce the continuation of the march – perhaps to the nearest inter-section and back, whereupon the event will either break up as people drift away, or be attacked by the police.

Those who attended the march will return home with bruises and blisters, but no better idea of what to do next than they had when they arrived. This is another way of saying that the entire exercise was wasted. The hard work applied by the organisers and the great potential provided by the enthusiasm of thousands is squandered.

The idea of a march followed by speeches is not inher-ently a bad one, as long as its purposes are kept in sight at every moment: to inspire, to inform, and then to direct the crowd to action, by which I mean a specific task rather than a vague call to 'rise up'. In every town, there are people who specialise in raising the energy of crowds: DJs and MCs at concerts and comedy clubs, motivational coaches, fitness instructors, bingo callers, sports commentators, auctioneers and chat show hosts. There is bound to be at least one person among them who is sympathetic to the cause.

In the weeks before the march, this energiser would sit down with the organisers and plan the event as carefully as the logistics have been planned. They would choose some musicians and a maximum of three speakers, all of whom possess the skill of holding an audience in the palm of their hand. The role of these speakers would not be to represent the groups that organised the march, but to explain the issues and the next steps to the audience. Once they had accepted the invitation, they would be carefully briefed about the aims of the demonstration and the messages that had to be conveyed.

The musicians would play as the crowd assembled, ensuring that nobody missed the speeches, which would now be a crucial component of the event. Then the energiser would use her or his skills to raise the level of excitement, before introducing the first speaker. The speakers would each have just a few minutes, and the final one would lay out in unequivocal terms what the audience was being asked to do. This would take the form of a request to perform a concrete action in the days or weeks that followed – generally a large and ambitious one. The energiser would bring back the musicians to lead the crowd in an anthem: there's no better way of generating a sense of solidarity and shared emotion.

The energiser would announce the end of the demonstration, reminding the audience of the next step they had been asked to take. The march might lead directly to this step – a planning meeting in a nearby building, for example – or stewards would line the exit points to take email addresses or to sign people up on the spot as volunteers for a specific task. In other words, the event would not be an end in itself, but would be overtly and specifically designed to support a wider programme.

Every step builds towards the next one, each combining to build towards the eventual aim of the campaign. Nothing is done without strategic thinking, no strategy is agreed without a set of tactics to implement it. No opportunities are wasted, no enthusiasm allowed to deflate. These are among the lessons of the Sanders campaign.

Indivisible

Now here is where the idea blossoms. Big Organising could be combined with the methods prescribed in the *Indivisible* guide to influencing Members of Congress, written by former congressional staffers.[3] These people studied the techniques developed by the Tea Party movement and extracted the key lessons (see below). Bring the two procedures together, and the impossible begins to look plausible.

Here is an example: a constitutional amendment introducing a fair campaign funding system to the United States, of the kind proposed by the campaign group Wolf-PAC.[4] That is about as big as political ambitions get, possibly the biggest political transformation in America since desegregation. Here, drawing together the work of Wolf-PAC, *Indivisible* and the Sanders campaign, is an idea of how a movement to secure an amendment could succeed.

First, a watertight constitutional amendment is drafted, with the help of sympathetic lawyers. Then the problems with the current system and the promise of a better one are explained in blog posts, articles and videos. Initial rallies and marches are held to raise the issue in people's minds, and build towards the next concrete actions.

Then Big Organising, using its proliferating, volunteer-led barnstorms, would allocate a national network of volunteers to phone-bank teams and doorstep canvassing. These volunteers would begin to contact Americans. Not some Americans, or most Americans, but every adult in the United States. They would raise the issue of how the whole damn system is bought and sold, and explain how the constitutional amendment could save US democracy and transform the life of the nation. They would make a specific request: they want people to speak to their Member of Congress, on the phone number provided, and press that Member to support the amendment.

At the same time, the *Indivisible* techniques would kick in. The volunteers, clustered in local groups, would lead the lobbying effort. They would not only ring and email their own Members, but visit their offices to speak to them in person, ideally bringing a well-known local figure with them, with the media in tow.

Campaigners would turn up at the public town hall events the Member holds, spread through the room and politely but trenchantly press the request that she or he support the amendment, with a series of focused and carefully phrased questions developed in advance. If the first questioner does not get a satisfactory reply, the next one builds on the previous question – in every case supported by the applause of the other volunteers in the audience. The exchanges are filmed and shared on social media and, if it will play the footage, on the established media.

This must be done peacefully and calmly, and the process should stop after a few such questions are asked. The meeting must not be hijacked: other people in the room have a democratic right to have their concerns heard, and the Member must also be able to speak. In this respect, we should distinguish ourselves from the Tea Party movement and other groups that have crossed the fine line between exercising their democratic rights, on one side, and bullying and harassment on the other. At no time, in campaigning of this kind, should we overlook the humanity of the person we are trying to reach. Whatever we might think of their politics, we must never forget that we are addressing a real person, whose feelings and perceptions of threat are likely to be similar to our own.

In this spirit, the campaigners appear at other public events the Member attends – parades, ribbon-cuttings and the rest – and raise the issue politely, visibly, but briefly, in front of the press and voters. More rallies and marches take place – now much bigger than before – amplifying the demand and moving people towards the next stages of the campaign.

As the movement builds, the Members start to sweat. On one hand, their funders (who until this point have been all-powerful), the party machine and the billionaire press are demanding that they hold firm. On the other, their constituents are taking up the cause in droves, and it is beginning to look like an election issue, perhaps *the* election issue. At some point the Members begin to perceive resistance to the amendment as more of an electoral liability than an asset.

One or two of them will break. As this happens, the campaigners use it as extra leverage over those who will not support the amendment: Why won't you follow suit? Are they braver than you are? Didn't we elect you to represent the people, not the money? The more Members peel off, the more exposed the remainder feel. And throughout all this, the phone banks are working, talking to every adult in the Union, and the phones in the Congressional offices are ringing off the hook. The pressure begins to look impossible to resist . . .

If this dam breaks, the political system goes with it. It is a revolutionary transformation from which many others will follow, in America and around the world. The US government, elected by means more plutocratic than democratic, wielding extraordinary power, has impeded progress towards a more generous, inclusive politics in global forums and in many other nations. If the current political funding system is swept away, this is the point at which everything changes.

And the same techniques can be used to rescue and reform our political systems in any nation that claims to be a democracy.

Unstoppable

The frustration that almost all those who want a kinder, better, more protective politics experience is that we know we have, in theory at least, the numbers on our side. Most people are socially minded, empathetic and altruistic. They would prefer to live in a world in which everyone is treated with respect and decency, and in which we do not squander either our own lives or the natural gifts on which our children and the rest of the living world depend. But a small handful, using lies and distractions and confusion, stifle this latent desire for change.

We know that, if we can mobilise such silent majorities, there is nothing this small minority can do to stop us. But because we have failed to understand what is possible, and above all failed to tell a new compelling story of transformation and restoration, our imagination has been truncated. As we begin to apprehend what can be done, we can extract ourselves from this trap. By allowing people to appreciate how powerful they are and how useful they can be, and how politics and government can belong to all of us rather than only a remote elite, we will become unstoppable.

Conclusion:
The Politics of Belonging

This book has sought to tell a story of hope and restoration, a story that might help to light a path towards a better world. Its purpose is to reveal the defining aspects of our nature. It seeks to revive our humanity – in both senses of this word.

At the beginning, I sketched the broad lines of this story. In subsequent chapters I explored some of the policies and strategies that could help to realise it. They now enable us to tell the tale again, drawing this time on experience, action and practical possibility. It goes like this.

The Longing for Belonging

We are extraordinary creatures, whose capacity for altruism and reciprocity is unmatched in the animal kingdom. But these remarkable traits have been suppressed by an ideology of extreme individualism and competition. With the help of this ideology, and the story used to project it, alienation and loneliness have become the defining conditions of our time. Far from apprehending them as threats to our well-being, we have been induced to see them as aspirations.

As a result, we find it hard to imagine our way out of the reaction and helplessness to which we have succumbed. We struggle to recognise, let alone resolve, our common problems. This has frustrated our potential to do what humans do best: to see a threat to one as a threat to all; to find common ground in confronting our predicaments; and to unite to overcome them.

To escape from this trap, we first need to perceive it. We need to name the power that has exacerbated our isolation and our collective loss of agency. This power is neoliberalism, the story it tells and the political programmes that arise from it. Our failure to tell a new story with which to replace it has allowed this power to persist and grow.

By confronting the politics of alienation with a politics of belonging, we rekindle our imagination and discover our power to act.

Good Fellowship

I have sought to describe a path that starts from where we are, rather than from where we might wish to be. It begins on our doorsteps, with an account of how we can build communities in which everyone can thrive.

Community projects proliferate into a vibrant, participatory culture that transforms the character of our neighbourhoods. New social and commercial enterprises strengthen our sense of attachment and ownership.

A flourishing community stimulates our innate urge to cooperate. It helps immunise us against extremism and demagoguery, and it turns democracy into a daily habit. Community is the place from which a new politics begins to grow.

The Common Weal

Communities come to own and manage local resources, ensuring that wealth is widely shared and that the sense of belonging to place and people is strengthened. Using common riches to fund universal benefits provides everyone with security and resilience. A kinder world stimulates and normalises our kinder values.

By gaining control of public investment, we take ownership of both our localities and our lives. We come to see ourselves as political agents, rather than as supplicants. These shifts help to embed a new economics, whose purpose is to allow us to thrive without destroying the Earth's living systems.

Owning the System

By reclaiming democratic power, we build a politics that belongs to all of us. A real democracy is one that allows the people to design the system. New methods and rules for elections ensure that every vote counts and that financial power can never vanquish political power.

Representative democracy is reinforced by a participatory democracy that allows us to refine our political choices. The tussle for sovereignty between parliament and people is resolved in favour of the people.

Global bodies that have seized power without a democratic mandate are either disbanded or democratised. Decision-making is returned to the smallest political units that can discharge it. Wherever power resides, it is accountable to the people, through election and participation. Power becomes a function of community.

The Wisdom of Crowds

Some of these proposals may sound like impossible dreams. But in Chapter 9 I explored the means by which they might be realised. Organising self-motivated networks of volunteers, using the wisdom of crowds to refine and enhance new political techniques, we mobilise a force that the power of money can never match: mutual aid, operating on a grand scale.

In combination with new strategies for reaching and persuading politicians, there may be nothing within the scope of democratic politics that this method cannot achieve, nothing that it cannot change.

Coming Home to Ourselves

Through restoring community, renewing civic life and claiming our place in the world, we build a society in which our extraordinary nature – our altruism, empathy and deep connection – is released.

When we emerge from the age of loneliness and alienation, from an obsession with competition and extreme individualism, from the worship of image and celebrity and power and wealth, we will find a person waiting for us. It is a person better than we might have imagined, whose real character has been suppressed. It is the one who lives inside us, who has been there all along.

Acknowledgements

I would never have started this book were it not for the persistence and persuasiveness of my editor at Verso, Leo Hollis. I suppose that, after publishing a book with him called *How Did We Get Into This Mess?*, it was inevitable that I would have to write one about how to get out of it. But while this was clear to him, it became clear to me only after he had deployed his considerable reserves of brutal charm.

Many were the days when I cursed the ridiculously tight deadline we had agreed, and the ebullient determination with which it was enforced. How often did I wonder how I had been persuaded, at the expense of sleep, sanity and family life, to succumb to his despotic regime? But he has the knack of making things happen without anyone being able to see how. And the world is a better place as a result.

I would never have been able to complete it were it not for the brilliance of my researcher, Charlie Young. His ability to map the political territory, his erudition and knowledge of who is doing what, and the speed and accuracy of his research have been a constant support to me. This is someone who will go far.

My agents James Macdonald Lockhart and Ant Harwood have, as always, been steadfast friends and supporters, helping me survive in a world for which I am manifestly ill-equipped. My assistants Ketty Hughes and Fiona Rowe have kept this world at bay with great panache, enabling me to spend every day lost in my abstractions and creations and speculations.

The help I received from friends and reviewers has transformed this book. George Marshall single-handedly turned it around, through his tutorials, via email and Skype, on narrative structure, framing and political persuasion. Kate Raworth and Roman Krznaric, as well as inspiring much of the content of the book, gave me crucial counsel on its structure and themes. While working on our album, *Breaking the Spell of Loneliness*, which we wrote and toured together, Ewan McLennan helped to form my views on alienation, loneliness and belonging. A thousand thanks to all of you.

I have been blessed with invaluable advice from some of the smartest thinkers I have encountered, who have either reviewed my book for me or have helped me explore the issues it covers or both. Danny Dorling, Bec Sanderson, Mark Lynas, Jeremy Gilbert, Bill McKibben, Stuart White, Eliane Glaser, Gar Alperovitz, Victoria Chick and the Post-Keynesian Economics Study Group, Sheila Jasanoff, James Gustave Speth, Beth Stratford, David Boyle, Pat Conaty, Gabriel Bristow, Noam Chomsky, Anna Schiffrin and Anthony Barnett: I owe them all a pint, and much more.

Thank you too to Ben Okri, Becky Bond, Zack Exley and

Neal Lawson for their generosity, and their magnificent work.

To other friends I'm permanently grateful: for their support and loving kindness and because I know they will always be there. Among them are Jony Easterby, Hannah Scrase, Ralph Collard, Jay Griffiths, Bruce Heagerty, Hugh Warwick, Zoe Broughton, Paul Kingsnorth, Adrian Arbib, Eleanor Monbiot, Caspar Henderson, Maria Padget, Annie Levy, John Vidal, Tamsin Hartley, Marieke Wrigley, Tony and Mieke Wrigley, Phil Bloomer, Ruth Mayne, Roger Harrabin, Mary Stockdale, Jon Corbett, Nick Totman, Matt Prescott, Dave and Aine Venables, Candy March, Allan Shepherd and other members of the Machynlleth Housing Co-op, Ted Oakes, Ritchie Tassell, Charmian Savile, David Rabey, Inez von Rege, Mike Parker, and Neil and Jayne Hopkins.

My wonderful and long-suffering editors at the *Guardian* have given me the space and freedom to explore many of the ideas that have crystallised in this book. Thank you to them as well.

And above all, thank you to my partner, Rebecca, who has put up with all this nonsense, and my daughters Hanna and Martha. Thank you for all the love and joy you give me.

Notes

1 A Story of Our Times

1 George Marshall, *Don't Even Think About It: Why Our Brains Are Wired to Ignore Climate Change* (London: Bloomsbury, 2015).

2 Shalom H. Schwartz, 'Basic Human Values: Theory, Measurement, and Applications', *Revue Française de Sociologie* 47: 4 (2006), at rfs-revue.com; Tom Crompton, 'Common Cause: The Case for Working with our Cultural Values', WWF-UK, September 2010, pdf at assets.wwf.org.uk; Kennon M. Sheldon and Charles P. Nichols, 'Comparing Democrats and Republicans on Intrinsic and Extrinsic Values', *Journal of Applied Social Psychology* 39: 3 (February 2009), at onlinelibrary.wiley.com.

3 Tim Kasser, 'Values and Human Wellbeing: The Bellagio Initiative', November 2011, at opendocs.ids.ac.uk.

4 Crompton, 'Common Cause'.

5 Tom Crompton, Rebecca Sanderson, Mike Prentice, Netta Weinstein, Oliver Smith and Tim Kasser, 'Perceptions Matter – Full Report: The Common Cause UK Values Survey', Common Cause Foundation, March 2016, at valuesandframes.org.

6 Wolfgang Bilsky, Anna K. Döring, Franka van Beeck, Isabel Rose, Johanna Schmitz, Katrin Aryus, Lisa Drögekamp and Jeannette Sindermann, 'Assessment of Children's Value Structures and Value Preferences', *Swiss Journal of Psychology* 72 (June 2013); Shalom Schwartz

and Anat Bardi, 'Value Hierarchies Across Cultures: Taking a Similarities Perspective', *Journal of Cross-Cultural Psychology* 32: 3 (May 2001).

7   Kennon M. Sheldon and Tim Kasser, 'Psychological Threat and Extrinsic Goal Striving', *Motivation and Emotion* 32: 1 (March 2008), pdf at selfdeterminationtheory.org.

8   Stefan Svallfors, 'Policy Feedback, Generational Replacement, and Attitudes to State Intervention: Eastern and Western Germany, 1990–2006', *European Political Science Review* 2: 1 (March 2010), at cambridge.org.

9   Crompton et al., 'Perceptions Matter'.

10   Alex Evans with a foreword by Tim Smit, *The Myth Gap: What Happens When Evidence and Arguments Aren't Enough?* (London: Eden Project, 2017).

11   Keith Jensen, Amrisha Vaish and Marco F. H. Schmidt, 'The Emergence of Human Prosociality: Aligning with Others through Feelings, Concerns, and Norms', *Frontiers in Psychology* 5 (July 2014), at journal.frontiersin.org.

12   C. Daniel Batson, *Altruism in Humans* (Oxford: Oxford University Press, 2011); Kristian Ove R. Myrseth and Conny E. Wollbrant, 'Models Inconsistent with Altruism Cannot Explain the Evolution of Human Cooperation', *Proceedings of the National Academy of Sciences of the United States* 113: 18 (May 2016), at pnas.org.

13   Felix Warneken and Michael Tomasello, 'Helping and Cooperation at 14 Months of Age', *Infancy* 11: 3 (May 2007), at onlinelibrary.wiley.com.

14   Federico Rossano, Hannes Rakoczy and Michael Tomasello, 'Young Children's Understanding of Violations of Property Rights', *Cognition* 121: 2 (November 2011), at sciencedirect.com.

15   Hynek Burda, Rodney L. Honeycutt, Sabine Begall, Oliver Locker-Grütjen and Andreas Scharff, 'Are Naked and Common Mole-Rats Eusocial and If So, Why?' *Behavioural Ecology and Sociobiology* 47: 5 (April 2000), at jstor.org.

16   Paolo Riva, James H. Wirth and Kipling D. Williams, 'The Consequences of Pain: The Social and Physical Pain Overlap on Psychological Responses', *European Journal of Psychology* 41: 6 (October 2011); Naomi I. Eisenberg, Johanna M. Jarcho, Matthew D. Lieberman and Bruce D. Naliboff, 'An Experimental Study of Shared Sensitivity to Physical Pain and Social Rejection', *International Association for the Study of Pain* 126: 1 (June 2006), pdf at scn.ucla.edu.

17   Franklin D. McMillan, 'The Psychobiology of Social Pain: Evidence for a Neurocognitive Overlap with Physical Pain and Welfare Implications for Social Animals with Special Attention to the Domestic Dog (*Canis familiaris*)', *Physiology and Behaviour* 167 (1 December 2016).

18   Naomi I. Eisenberger and Matthew D. Lieberman, 'Why It Hurts to Be Left Out: The Neurocognitive Overlap Between Physical and Social Pain', in *The Social Outcast: Ostracism, Social Exclusion, Rejection, and Bullying* (New York: Psychology Press, 2014), pdf at scn.ucla.edu.

19   Johann Hari, *Chasing the Scream: The First and Last Days of the War on Drugs* (New York: Bloomsbury, 2016).

20   See Shaun Gallagher, 'The Cruel and Unusual Phenomenology of Solitary Confinement', *Frontiers in Psychology* 5: 585 (May 2014).

21   Natalie Gil, 'Loneliness: A Silent Plague that Is Hurting Young People', *Guardian*, 20 July 2014.

22   Jenny Edwards and Paul Farmer, 'The Most Terrible Poverty: Loneliness and Mental Health', Campaign to End Loneliness, 16 June 2014, at campaigntoendloneliness.org.

23   Stephanie Cacioppo, John P. Capitanio and John T. Cacioppo, 'Toward a Neurology of Loneliness', *Psychology Bulletin* 140: 6 (November 2014), pdf at static1.squarespace.com.

24   Nicole K. Valtorta, Mona Kanaan, Simon Gilbody, Sara Ronzi and Barbara Hanratty, 'Loneliness and Social Isolation as Risk Factors for Coronary Heart Disease and Stroke: Systemic Review and Meta-analysis of Longitudinal Observational Studies', *Heart* 102: 3 (November 2014).

25   Cacioppo et al., 'Toward a Neurology of Loneliness'.

26   Julianne Holt-Lunstad, Timothy B. Smith and J. Bradley Layton, 'Social Relationships and Mortality Risk: A Meta-analytic Review', *PLOS Medicine* 7: 7 (July 2010).

27   Claire Niedzwiedz, 'Loneliness Is an Issue of Inequality', Centre for Research on Environment, Society and Health, 28 July 2016, at cresh.org.uk.

28   Graeme Wood, 'Secret Fears of the Super Rich', *Atlantic*, April 2011.

29   Rory Carroll, 'We Need Human Interaction: Meet the LA Man Who Walks People for a Living', *Guardian*, 14 September 2016.

30   Chris Colin, 'The Incredibly True Story of Renting a Friend in Tokyo', Afar, 19 February 2016, at afar.com.

31   Deborah Hardoon, 'An Economy for the 99%: It's Time to Build a Human Economy that Benefits Everyone, Not Just the Privileged Few', Oxfam, January 2017, at policy-practice.oxfam.org.uk.

32   This process is described in Kate Raworth, *Doughnut Economics: Seven Ways to Think Like a 21st Century Economist* (White River Junction, VT: Chelsea Green, 2017).

33   Jensen et al., 'The Emergence of Human Prosociality'.

34 Fred L. Block and Margaret R. Somers, *The Power of Market Fundamentalism: Karl Polyani's Critique* (Cambridge, MA: Harvard University Press, 2014).

35 Roberto Stefan Foa and Yascha Mounk, 'The Signs of Deconsolidation', *Journal of Democracy* 28: 1 (January 2017), pdf at journalofdemocracy. org.

36 Thomas Paine, *Rights of Man: Being an Answer to Mr Burke's Attack on the French Revolution* (London: Watts, 1791).

37 Edmund Burke, *Reflections on the Revolution in France: And on the Proceedings in Certain Societies in London Relative to that Event* (London: J. Dodsley, 1790).

2 A Captive Audience

1 Daniel Stedman Jones, *Masters of the Universe: Hayek, Friedman, and the Birth of Neoliberal Politics* (Princeton, NJ: Princeton University Press, 2014).

2 Friedrich A. von Hayek, *The Road to Serfdom* (London: Routledge, 1944).

3 David Harvey, *A Brief History of Neoliberalism* (Oxford: Oxford University Press, 2011).

4 Stedman Jones, *Masters of the Universe*.

5 Friedrich A. von Hayek, *The Constitution of Liberty* (London: Routledge & Kegan Paul, 1960).

6 Stedman Jones, *Masters of the Universe*.

7 Madsen Pirie, *Think Tank: The Story of the Adam Smith Institute* (New York: Biteback, 2012).

8 Arthur C. Brooks, 'Margaret Thatcher Was a Powerful Voice for Free Enterprise and Liberty', American Enterprise Institute, 8 April 2013, at aei.org.

9 Sky News, 'Margaret Thatcher Pursued Welfare Cut Plans Despite Public Outcry', 25 November 2016, at news.sky.com.

10 Paul Verhaeghe and J. A. Hedley-Prole, *What About Me? The Struggle for Identity in a Market-Based Society* (Melbourne: Scribe, 2016).

11 Andrew Sayer, *Why We Can't Afford the Rich* (Bristol: Policy Press, 2016).

12 Greg Gandin, 'The Road From Serfdom', *Counterpunch*, 17 November 2006, at counterpunch.org.

13 This comparison was made by Isaiah Berlin in his 1958 lecture, *Two Concepts of Liberty*.

14 Ludwig von Mises, *Bureaucracy* (New Haven, CT: Yale University Press, 1944).

15   Sayer, *Why We Can't Afford the Rich*.

16   Thomas Piketty, *Capital in the Twenty-First Century* (Cambridge, MA: Harvard University Press, 2014).

17   Aditya Chakrabortty, 'Rail Privatisation: Legalised Larceny', *Guardian*, 4 November 2013.

18   Tony Judt, *Ill Fares the Land* (New York: Penguin, 2010).

19   Chris Hedges, 'The Revenge of the Lower Classes and the Rise of American Fascism', *Truthdig*, 8 August 2016, at truthdig.com.

20   George Monbiot, 'How Big Tobacco's Lobbyists Get What They Want from the Media', *Guardian*, 17 March 2014.

21   George Monbiot, 'The Tea Party Movement: Deluded and Inspired by Billionaires', *Guardian*, 25 October 2010.

22   Jane Mayer, *Dark Money: The Hidden History of the Billionaires Behind the Rise of the Radical Right* (New York: Anchor, 2017).

3 Don't Look Back

1   John Maynard Keynes, *The General Theory of Employment, Interest and Money* (London: Macmillan, 1936).

2   John Reed, 'Mixed Response Greets Car-Scrapping Bonus', *Financial Times*, 23 April 2009.

3   George Monbiot, 'Scrap It', *Guardian*, 10 March 2009.

4   Rawi Abdelal, *Capital Rules: The Construction of Global Finance* (Cambridge, MA: Harvard University Press, 2007).

5   James D. Ward, Paul C. Sutton, Adrian D. Werner, Robert Costanza, Steve M. Mohr and Craig T. Simmons, 'Is Decoupling GDP Growth from Environmental Impact Possible?' *PLOS ONE* 11: 10 (October 2016), at journals.plos.org.

6   Dick Morris, *Behind the Oval Office: Winning the Presidency in the Nineties* (New York: Random House, 1997).

7   Jill Abramson, 'The Clintons Turned the Democratic Party Over to Donors. Can It Recover?' *Guardian*, 21 December 2016.

8   Franklin D. Roosevelt, 'Message to Congress on Curbing Monopolies', 1938, at presidency.ucsb.edu.

9   Louis D. Brandeis Legacy Fund for Social Justice, at brandeis.edu.

10   Matt Stoller, 'Democrats Can't Win Until They Recognize How Bad Obama's Financial Policies Were', *Washington Post*, 12 January 2017.

11   Emmanuel Saez, 'Striking It Richer: The Evolution of Top Incomes in the United States', Institute for Research on Labour and Employment, UC Berkeley, September 2013, pdf at eml.berkeley.edu.

12 Anushka Asthana and Rowena Mason, 'Barack Obama: Brexit Would Put UK "Back of the Queue" for Trade Talks', *Guardian*, 22 April 2016.

13 Charlotte Alter, 'Voter Turnout in Midterm Elections Hits 72-Year Low', *Time*, 10 November 2014.

14 Nicholas Confessore and Steve Eder, 'In Hacked DNC Emails, a Glimpse of How Big Money Works', *New York Times*, 25 July 2016.

15 'Labour Party Manifesto', 2015, pdf at labour.org.uk.

16 YouGov, 'The Times Survey Results', 18–19 April 2017, https://d25d2506sfb94s.cloudfront.net/cumulus_uploads/document/04xxn42p3e/TimesResults_170419_VI_Trackers_GE_W.pdf.

17 John Curtice, 'Local Elections 2017: Six Key Lessons for the General Election', BBC.com, 5 May 2017.

4 Alienation

1 '2017 Edelman Trust Barometer: Global Annual Study', at edelman.com.

2 George Bernard Shaw, *Major Barbara* (London: Constable, 1905).

3 Tony Judt, *Ill Fares the Land* (New York: Penguin, 2010).

4 Donald Appleyard, *Liveable Streets* (Berkeley, CA: University of California Press, 1981); Joshua Hart and Graham Peter Pankhurst, 'Driven To Excess: Impacts of Motor Vehicles on the Quality of Life of Residents of Three Streets in Bristol, UK', *World Transport Policy and Practice* 17: 2 (January 2011), pdf at eprints.uwe.ac.uk.

5 'Typical Earnings of the Self-Employed Lower than 20 Years Ago', press release, Resolution Foundation, 18 October 2016, at resolutionfoundation.org.

6 Byung-Chul Han, 'Why Revolution Is No Longer Possible', Open Democracy, 23 October 2015, at opendemocracy.net.

7 Yalda T. Uhls and Patricia M. Greenfield, 'The Rise of Fame: An Historical Content Analysis', *Cyberpsychology* 5: 1 (November 2011), at cyberpsychology.eu.

8 Nick Couldry and Tim Markham, 'Celebrity Culture and Public Connection: Bridge or Chasm?', *International Journal of Cultural Studies* 10: 4 (December 2007), pdf at eprints.lse.ac.uk.

9 Rhiannon Lucy Cosslett, 'Thinner, Smoother, Better: In the Era of Retouching, That's What Girls Have to Be', *Guardian*, 8 September 2016.

10 Yalda T. Uhls, Eleni Zgourou and Patricia M. Greenfield, '21st Century Media, Fame, and Other Future Aspirations: A National Survey of 9–15 Year Olds', *Cyberpsychology* 8: 4 (December 2014), at cyberpsychology.eu.

11   Monika A. Bauer, James E. B. Wilkie, Jung K. Kim and Galen V. Bodenhausen, 'Cuing Consumerism: Situational Materialism Undermines Personal and Social Well-Being', *Psychological Science* 23: 5 (March 2012).

12   Pankaj Mishra, *Age of Anger: A History of the Present* (New York: Farrar, Straus & Giroux, 2017).

13   Anne Amnesia, 'Unnecessariat: More Crows than Eagles' (blog entry), 10 May 2016, at morecrows.wordpress.com.

14   Hannah Arendt, *The Origins of Totalitarianism* (New York: Harcourt, Brace & World, 1968).

15   Daniel Pauly, 'Anecdotes and the Shifting Baseline Syndrome of Fisheries', *Trends in Ecology and Evolution* 10: 10 (October 1995), at sciencedirect.com.

5 Belonging

1   Kimberley Brownlee, *Social Rights* (London: Oxford University Press, forthcoming).

2   David Prynn, 'The Clarion Clubs, Rambling and the Holiday Associations in Britain since the 1890s', *Journal of Contemporary History* 11: 2–3.

3   Ibid.

4   Ronald Butt, 'Margaret Thatcher', *Sunday Times*, 1 May 1981, available at margaretthatcher.org.

5   Surbiton: a London suburb. Jeremy Gilbert, 'Why Did "Working-Class Culture" Disintegrate in the 1980s? A Sort of Reply to Paul Mason', *Open Democracy*, 18 April 2016, at opendemocracy.net.

6   Timebanking UK, at timebanking.org.

7   The Food Assembly, at thefoodassembly.com.

8   Transition Network, at transitionnetwork.org.

9   Men's Sheds, at menssheds.org.uk.

10   Sunday Assembly, at sundayassembly.com.

11   Playing Out, at playingout.net.

12   Playing Out, 'The Impact of Playing Out', n.d., at playingout.net.

13   Adele Peters, 'Here's What Happened When a Neighbourhood Decided to Ban Cars for a Month', *Fast Company*, 11 May 2015, at fastcompany.com.

14   Open Works research project, 'Designed to Scale: Mass Participation to Build Resilient Communities', August 2015, at issuu.com.

15   Athlyn Cathcart-Keays, 'In Nottingham, One Woman Is Fighting Food Poverty with "Social Eating" ', *Guardian*, 17 February 2015.

16   Open Works, 'Designed to Scale'.

17 Knowledge Networks and Insight Policy Research, 'Loneliness among Older Adults: A National Survey of Adults 45+', ARRP, September 2010, pdf at assets.aarp.org.

18 Karin van Rooij, 'De Makers van Rotterdam #2: Maurice Specht over de Leeszaal Rotterdam West. Vers Beton', *Vers Beton*, 30 January 2013, at versbeton.nl.

19 Open Works, 'Designed to Scale'.

20 Annah MacKenzie, 'Estonoesunsolar: Finding Opportunity in Emptiness in Zaragoza, Spain', Project for Public Spaces, 28 May 2015, at pps.org.

21 Incredible Edible, at incredible-edible-todmorden.co.uk.

22 Christopher H. Achen and Larry M. Bartels, *Democracy for Realists: Why Elections Do Not Produce Responsive Government* (Princeton/Oxford: Princeton University Press, 2016).

23 Dan Kahan, 'Fixing the Communications Failure', *Nature* 463: 7,279 (January 2010).

24 '2017 Edelman Trust Barometer', at edelman.com.

25 Mike Davis, 'Who Will Build The Ark?', *New Left Review* II/61 (January–February 2010).

26 Community Environmental Legal Defense Fund, at celdf.org.

27 The World Cafe, at theworldcafe.com.

28 Paul Mason, *PostCapitalism: A Guide to Our Future* (London: Penguin, 2016).

6 Our Economy

1 Paul A. Samuelson, *Economics* (New York: McGraw-Hill, 1973).

2 David Bollier and Silke Helfrich, *Patterns of Commoning* (Amherst, MA: Commons Strategies Group/Off the Common Books, 2015).

3 Garrett Hardin, 'The Tragedy of the Commons', *Science* 162: 3,859 (December 1968).

4 Elinor Ostrom, *Governing the Commons: The Evolution of Institutions for Collective Action* (Cambridge: Cambridge University Press, 1990).

5 George Monbiot, 'Academic Publishers Make Murdoch Look Like a Socialist', *Guardian*, 29 August 2011.

6 April Glaser, 'Net Neutrality Faces Extinction under Trump', Recode, 12 December 2016, at recode.net.

7 George Lakey, *Viking Economics: How the Scandinavians Got It Right and How We Can, Too* (New York: Melville House, 2017).

8 Stacco Troncoso, Ann Marie Utratel, Michel Bauwens (eds) 'Commons Transition: Policy Proposals for an Open Knowledge Commons Society', P2P Foundation, June 2014, pdf at commonstransition.org.

9 Paul Mason, *PostCapitalism: A Guide to Our Future* (London: Penguin, 2016).

10 Thomas Paine, 'Agrarian Justice' (1795), pdf at piketty.pse.ens.fr.

11 Land Value Taxation Campaign, 'Winston Churchill Said It All Better than We Can', 14 February 2010, at landvaluetax.org.

12 Martin Adams, *Land: A New Paradigm for a Thriving World* (Berkeley, CA: North Atlantic, 2015).

13 Adam Smith, *An Inquiry into the Nature and Causes of the Wealth of Nations* (London: T & J Allman, 1776).

14 Carol M. Rose, 'The Several Futures of Property: Of Cyberspace and Folk Tales, Emission Trades and Ecosystems', Faculty Scholarship Series, Paper 1804 (January 1998), at digitalcommons.law.yale.edu.

15 Peter Barnes, 'Common Wealth Trusts: Structures of Transition', Great Transition Initiative, August 2015, at greattransition.org.

16 Oliver Tickell, *Kyoto 2: How to Manage the Global Greenhouse* (London/ New York: Zed, 2008).

17 Angela Cummine, *Citizens' Wealth: Why (and How) Sovereign Funds Should be Managed by the People for the People* (New Haven, CT: Yale University Press, 2016); Stewart Lansley, *A Sharing Economy: How Social Wealth Funds can Reduce Inequality and Help Balance the Books* (Bristol: Policy Press, 2016).

18 Thomas Pogge, 'Eradicating Systemic Poverty: Brief for a Global Resources Dividend', *Journal of Human Development* 2: 1 (January 2001).

19 Austin Douillard, 'US/Kenya: New Study Published on Results of Basic Income Pilot in Kenya', Basic Income Earth Network, 27 March 2017, at basicincome.org.

20 SEWA Bharat, 'A Little More, How Much It Is . . . Piloting Basic Income Transfers in Madhya Pradesh, India', UNICEF, January 2014, pdf at unicef.in.

21 Matt Zwolinski, Michael Huemer, Jim Manzi and Robert H. Frank, 'Basic Income and the Welfare State', Cato Unbound, August 2014, at cato-unbound.org.

22 Paine, 'Agrarian Justice'.

23 Martin Sandbu, 'The Tobin Tax Explained', *Financial Times*, 28 September 2011.

24 Yanis Varoufakis, 'The Universal Right to Capital Income', Project Syndicate, 31 October 2016, at project-syndicate.org.

7 Framing the Economy

1 Carla Ravaioli, *Economists and the Environment* (London: Zed, 1995).

2 Jonathan Wentworth, 'Securing UK Soil Health', Parliamentary Office of Science and Technology, August 2015, at researchbriefings.parliament.uk.

3   Chris Arsenault, 'Only 60 Years of Farming Left if Soil Degradation Continues', *Scientific American*, 6 December 2014.

4   R. J. Rickson, L. K. Deeks, A. Graves, J. A. H. Harris, M. G. Kibblewhite and R. Sakrabani, 'Input Constraints to Food Production: The Impact of Soil Degradation', *Food Security* 7: 2 (April 2015).

5   Friedrich A. von Hayek, *The Constitution of Liberty* (London: Routledge & Kegan Paul, 1960).

6   'Space Settlements: Spreading Life through the Solar System', at settlement.arc.nasa.gov.

7   Baby Bangs! Made Just for Little Girls, at baby-bangs.com.

8   Quirky Egg Minder Wink App Enabled Smart Egg Tray, at amazon.com.

9   Egg Scrambler – Hand Powered 'In-Shell' Egg Shaker Scrambles Eggs Without Breaking the Shell, at amazon.com.

10 Martin Croucher, 'Snow Room Is the Hot New Thing in UAE', *The National*, 27 September 2015.

11 Serkan Toto, 'Portable Watermelon Cooler', Tech Crunch, 19 July 2010, at techcrunch.com.

12 PetBot, at petbot.com.

13 Kate Raworth, *Doughnut Economics: Seven Ways to Think Like a 21st Century Economist* (White River Junction, VT: Chelsea Green, 2017).

14 George Lakoff, *Don't Think of an Elephant! Know Your Values and Frame the Debate* (White River Junction, VT: Chelsea Green, 2014).

15 Katrine Marçal, *Who Cooked Adam Smith's Dinner? A Story about Women and Economics* (London: Portobello, 2016).

16 Cited in Raworth, *Doughnut Economics*.

17 'UN Sustainable Development Goals: 17 Goals to Transform Our World', at un.org.

18 Stockholm Resilience Centre, 'The Nine Planetary Boundaries', at stockholmresilience.org.

19 Robert Costanza, Gar Alperovitz, Herman E. Daly, Joshua Farley, Carol Franco, Tim Jackson, Ida Kubiszewski, Juliet Schor and Peter Victor, 'Building a Sustainable and Desirable Economy-in-Society-in-Nature', United Nations Division for Sustainable Development, New York, 2012, pdf at epubs.surrey.ac.uk.

20 Josh Ryan-Collins, Tony Greenham, Leander Bindewald and Ludwig Schuster, 'Energising Money', New Economics Foundation, February 2013, at action.neweconomics.org.

21 Participatory Budget Project, 'PB Map & Process List', at participatorybudgeting.org.

22 Sónia Gonçalves, 'The Effects of Participatory Budgeting on Municipal

Expenditures and Infant Mortality in Brazil', *World Development* 53 (January 2014).

23 Brandon Jordan, 'How Communities Are Using Direct Democracy to Shape City Budgets', *Waging Non-Violence*, 28 September 2016, at wagingnonviolence.org.

24 Christopher H. Achen and Larry M. Bartels, *Democracy for Realists: Why Elections Do Not Produce Responsive Government* (Oxford: Princeton University Press, 2016).

25 Phil Byrne, 'Put People in Charge of Their Taxes and What Happens?', Friends of the Earth, 12 August 2015, at foe.co.uk.

8 Our Politics

1 Allan Smith, 'Global Security Expert: Yes, a President Can Unilaterally Decide to Launch a Nuclear Weapon', *UK Business Insider*, 22 December 2016.

2 Seth Ackerman, 'A Blueprint for a New Party', *Jacobin*, 8 November 2016, at jacobinmag.com.

3 Thomas Ferguson, Paul Jorgensen and Jie Chen, 'How Money Drives US Congressional Elections: More Evidence', Institute for New Economic Thinking, April 2015, pdf at ineteconomics.org.

4 Ibid.

5 George Monbiot, 'Frightened by Donald Trump? You Don't Know the Half of It', *Guardian*, 30 November 2016.

6 George Monbiot 'How Corporate Dark Money Is Taking Power on Both Sides of the Atlantic', *Guardian*, 2 February 2017.

7 James Madison, 'The Utility of the Union as a Safeguard Against Domestic Faction and Insurrection', *Daily Advertiser*, 22 November 1787, at constitution.org.

8 Andrew Mell, Simon Radford and Seth Alexander Thevoz, 'Is There a Market for Peerages? Can Donations Buy You a British Peerage? A Study in the Link Between Party Political Funding and Peerage Nominations, 2005–14', Department of Economics Discussion Paper Series, Ref. 744, at economics.ox.ac.uk.

9 Doug Cowan, 'Does Proportional Representation Give Too Much Power to Small Parties?', Electoral Reform Society, 23 June 2015, at electoral-reform.org.uk.

10 Stuart White, 'Parliaments, Constitutional Conventions, and Popular Sovereignty', *Journal of Politics and International Relations*, March 2017.

11 'Same Sex Marriage Referendum: National Summary Results', at rte.ie.

12 Scott E. Page, *The Difference: How the Power of Diversity Creates Better*

Groups, Firms, Schools, and Societies (Princeton, NJ: Princeton University Press, 2008).

13   Patrick Fournier and Henk Van Der Halk, *When Citizens Decide: Lessons from Citizen Assemblies on Electoral Reform* (Oxford: Oxford University Press, 2011).

14   Alan Renwick, 'How to Design a Constitutional Convention for the UK', Open Democracy, 23 September 2014, at opendemocracy.net.

15   Keith Sutherland, *A People's Parliament: A (Revised) Blueprint for a Very English Revolution* (Exeter: Imprint Academic, 2008).

16   Electoral Reform Society, 'Single Transferable Vote (STV)', at electoral-reform.org.uk.

17   OECD, 'Public Governance: A Matter of Trust', at oecd.org.

18   AIDA, 'Switzerland: Asylum Reform Approved by Referendum', Asylum Information Database, 6 August 2016, at asylumineurope.org.

19   Simon Geissbühler, 'Does Direct Democracy Really Work? A Review of the Empirical Evidence from Switzerland', *Polish Political Science Quarterly* 1: 1 (September 2013).

20   Julie Simon, Theo Bass, Victoria Boelman and Geoff Mulgan, 'Digital Democracy: The Tools Transforming Political Engagement, Nesta, February 2017, pdf at nesta.org.uk.

21   Nesta, 'vTaiwan Was Designed as a Neutral Platform to Engage Experts and Relevant Members in Large-Scale Engagement on Controversial Policy Issues', at nesta.org.uk.

22   Nesta, 'The e-Democracia Portal Aims to Make Legislation More Transparent to Citizens, by Embedding Digital Democracy in the National Parliament', at nesta.org.uk.

23   Simon et al., 'Digital Democracy'.

24   Melanie Swan, *Blockchain: Blueprint For a New Economy* (Sebastopol, CA: O'Reilly, 2015).

25   Marcella Atzori, 'Blockchain Technology and Decentralized Governance: Is the State Still Necessary?', University College of London, Center for Blockchain Technologies, December 2015, at papers.ssrn.com.

26   Joe Mitchell, 'Germany Has a Publicly Funded Agency with a Mission to Strengthen Democracy. The UK Needs One Too', at joe-mitchell.com.

27   Christian Beck, 'Further Insights from the German-Speaking Countries – the Voting Advice Applications Wahl-O-Mat, Wahlkabine and Smartvote', Democracy One Day, 13 February 2013, at democracyoneday.com.

28   Ibid.

29   George Monbiot, *The Age of Consent: A Manifesto for a New World Order* (London: Flamingo, 2003).

30   Debora MacKenzie, 'End of Nations: Is There an Alternative to Countries?', *New Scientist*, 4 September 2014.

31   Paul Arbair, '#Brexit, the Populist Surge and the Crisis of Complexity', 5 July 2015, at paularbair.wordpress.com.

9 Making It Happen

1   Aaron Blake, 'Here are the Latest, Most Damaging Things in the DNC's Leaked Emails', *Washington Post*, 25 July 2016.
2   Becky Bond and Zack Exley, *Rules for Revolutionaries: How Big Organizing Can Change Everything* (White River Junction, VT: Chelsea Green, 2016).
3   'Indivisible: A Practical Guide for Resisting the Trump Agenda', at indivisibleguide.com.
4   See wolf-pac.com.

Index